Praise for
In Search of the Proverbs 31 Man

"Michelle McKinney Hammond never wastes even a second of your time. She skirts no issues, never runs from controversy, and consistently engages her readers in authentic and entertaining dialog. She is so quick-witted, outrageously funny, and she holds your attention from start to finish. This is one of her most perceptive books. It's right on the mark. It goes to the heart of the ever-present man-woman debate, and it weighs in on the side of truth, of what works, and of what it takes to build a satisfying relationship that will last a lifetime. She speaks strongly to men, and she speaks just as strongly to women. As a seasoned clinical psychologist, I find her ideas highly stimulating and unusually helpful."

—NEIL CLARK WARREN, PH.D., founder of eHarmony.com

"Men, if you want to become a truly godly man and husband, *In Search of the Proverbs 31 Man* is a must-read. Women, if you want to know what to look for and nurture in a lifelong mate, this book is for you, too."

—DR. GREG SMALLEY, president and CEO of Smalley
Relationship Center

"Who isn't in search of the Proverbs 31 man? This book is for singles who want to know what character qualities are a must in a mate; for men who are confused by our culture and want to know what kind of man God esteems; and for women, tired of pressuring their men, who want to find the freedom of being a helper and soul mate. Michelle McKinney Hammond helps us discover the power of a   is willing to do it God's way."

—JAN FRANK, speaker and cc

"Michelle McKinney Hammond tells it like it is without pretense or sugar-coating. In her own unique style, she relays simple truths concerning the essence of masculinity from God's perspective. Every man wants to be ideal, but not many know what it takes to be *God's* ideal man. *In Search of the Proverbs 31 Man* identifies God's heartbeat concerning men. It points out the fact that a false understanding of manhood can be damaging not only to the individual but to those for whom he cares a great deal. This book shows you that the Proverbs 31 man is *not* damaged goods; instead, he's a polished diamond in the eyes of the Great Diamond Maker."

—DR. CREFLO A. DOLLAR, CEO of World Changers
Ministries and author of *The Successful Family*

IN SEARCH *of the* PROVERBS 31 MAN

IN SEARCH *of the* PROVERBS 31 MAN

THE ONE GOD APPROVES AND A WOMAN WANTS

MICHELLE
McKINNEY HAMMOND

WATERBROOK
PRESS

In Search of the Proverbs 31 Man
Published by WaterBrook Press
12265 Oracle Boulevard, Suite 200
Colorado Springs, CO 80921

ISBN: 978-1-57856-451-4

Published in association with the literary agency of Alive Communications, Inc., 7680 Goddard Street, Suite 200, Colorado Springs, CO 80920.

Published in the United States by WaterBrook Multnomah, an imprint of the Crown Publishing Group, a division of Random House Inc., New York.

WATERBROOK and its deer colophon are registered trademarks of Random House Inc.

Library of Congress Cataloging-in-Publication Data
McKinney Hammond, Michelle, 1957–
    In search of the Proverbs 31 man : the one God approves and a woman wants / Michelle McKinney Hammond.— 1st ed.
        p. cm.
    ISBN 1-57856-451-4
    1. Men in the Bible. 2. Man-woman relationships—Biblical teaching. 3. Christian men—Religious life. 4. Husbands—Religious life. I. Title.
    BS574.5.M35 2003
    248.8'42—dc21

                                                                2003011779

Printed in the United States of America
2010

15 14 13 12

To my fathers, Mr. George Hammond and Mr. William McKinney,
how blessed I am to have two incredible men in my life
to set the standard for the significant man in my life to follow.
I love you more than words can say.

———

To Uncle "Daddy" Stanley and Uncle Frank,
my two special loves, you make it hard for me
to give my heart to another (smile).

———

To Apostle Luther Blackwell, Frank Wilson, and Joel Brooks,
"father," brother, and friend, three men of God
who have had a profound impact on my life
in example and in word. It is because of you
that I always have hope for the men of the world.
You have shown me what God's design for man looks like,
and it is beautiful.

———

To my brothers, Ian, Okuru, and Nanapiah,
you have my heart as only brothers can.
It is my prayer that you become all
that God intended you to be.
You are well on your way.

CONTENTS

ACKNOWLEDGMENTS

My WaterBrook family, thank you for stretching me and making me dig deeper. John Hamilton, you are the best! Thanks for making me look good. Erin Healy, words cannot express how much I appreciate you. If I tried, you'd probably have to clean it up for me! Laura Wright, thank you for always seconding the motion for perfection—or as close as we can come to it. Chip MacGregor, your prayers as well as your counsel are priceless.

IDENTITY IN CRISIS

Someone—I think it was a bitter woman—once said, "Men! Can't live with them, can't kill them!" I have my own version of this expression: "Men! Can't live without them, though sometimes living with them may take a bit of work." But let's face it, most men would say the same thing about dealing with women!

Ladies and gentlemen, I must confess that I am grieved. As I travel around the country and speak with both men and women, I have seen that our struggle to find lasting love and nurturing relationships is at an all-time high. The men are confused. They no longer know what women want or need from them. The women are disappointed and frustrated. They always ask the same questions: "Where are the men?" "What is wrong with them?" "Why are they not able to commit?" "Why are they such wimps?"

I assure you up front that I have not set out to write a man-bashing book. Instead, I hope to champion God's original design for a man's life. I hope to encourage men and women alike with the following truth: Though perfection in any gender cannot be achieved this side of heaven, worthy efforts can be made with the help of the Holy Spirit. Why is this so important? Because we women need real men in our lives. And because God needs real men in His service.

Let's consider for a moment the crisis that threatens relationships between men and women today. A famous feminist once said that women have become the men they desire. Eww! Why? Perhaps because the world has distorted our roles and perspectives on gender traits. In our politically correct efforts to create a world of equality, we have created instead a great big tangled ball of yarn, with the liberating strand eluding us. We have lost sight of the God-given, unique strengths we have to offer each other as men and women.

As women have become more independent, self-sufficient, and powerful in the business world, I believe many have accepted the subtle lie that they no longer need men. The men, not knowing what is expected of them any longer, have largely abdicated (or been forced to resign) their posts as leaders, protectors, and providers.

On the other hand, the "every woman can be her own island" mentality is hard to sustain. Women have begun to groan under the weight of all they're doing and wonder why men no longer step up to the plate. Weariness has set in. So has compromise. For the sake of having a man, countless women have begun to settle for a new, watered-down version of manhood. Yet these women long for more. Not realizing that low expectations of men further perpetuate the downward trend, women sigh, "Oh well, men just aren't what they used to be."

I beg to differ. I believe that in the heart of every man is a desire to be the man his spirit knows he was created to be. Yet staggering numbers of men fear rejection, and so they settle for far less than what is required of them. Even so, these same men subconsciously resent women, who in their eyes have stripped them of their manhood. A man in such a position digs in his heels. He determines that the ultimate revenge for being backed into a corner by a strong woman is to let her flail just to prove she'd have been better off if she'd let him handle things in the first place.

THE GREAT MAN BEHIND THE GREAT WOMAN

In truth, women don't want to handle all of life on their own. Though doing everything faster than a speeding bullet, hurdling all aspects of life in a single bound, and leaping over tall dilemmas sounds admirable, none of us is Superwoman. The average woman gets stressed just *reading* about the virtuous woman so highly praised in Proverbs 31.

We've heard so much about the Proverbs 31 woman. She could bring home the bacon, fry it up in a pan, and never let her husband forget he's a man—all in one day. This chapter on her life has caused many a woman to have a serious inferiority complex. I've long made peace with her, understanding Proverbs 31 as a synopsis of her entire life, not an average week at her house. I hope that bit of good news will set you women free also.

The man behind this woman, however, has continually intrigued me. Who was he anyway? How did he feel about all this stuff his wife did? The proverb tells us in verse 28 that he praised her. He sounds like a pretty confident man. In fact, in verses 11 and 23, it says he was successful himself and not threatened by this entrepreneurial woman. Hmmm.

What part did he play in nurturing the kind of woman his wife became? How did he help establish the pleasant order that governed in his home? What was it about him that made others think so highly of him? What attributes did he display that filled his wife with confidence about their future, both financially and emotionally (verses 21,25)? What did he do that made her so infused with love for him that she diligently watched over all the matters of their household to make it a haven for him (verses 12,15,27)?

As I have pondered these questions, a list of attributes drawn from various men in the Bible has emerged in my mind and spirit concerning this mysterious man. The data forms a composite portrait of him. This strong man had not only the respect of his wife and his community but the approval of God as well. He did not diminish the strength of his wife; he supported it, and in so doing, he created a strong family unit that was a tribute to God's design for marriage. I believe God wants to forge these attributes in the heart of every man. The many faces from that composite of the Proverbs 31 man will form the foundation for the chapters to come.

DIAMONDS IN THE ROUGH

Why have I written this book? Because I love men. Some of my richest friendships have been with men. Some of the wisest and soundest counsel I have received over the course of my life has come from male friends and brothers who have served up the truth to me as completely and gently as possible. I've listened to them as they've struggled with their own issues, whether in careers or in love or in simply understanding what it means to be a man today. I've discovered that they feel things deeply without always believing they have permission to voice those feelings. I have been processing their confusion, frustration, and pain, and I believe I have some insights to help ease it.

Men, I want to show you what God's Word says you need to be. After receiving so many mixed signals from women and culture, who knows what is ideal? You've been told to be hard, soft, strong, sensitive, macho, kind, tough, and the list of contradiction goes on, to everyone's bemusement. If you're scratching your head and trying to figure out what women really want, well…I'm going to make it plain.

Between what God requires and what women desire, we have a lot of ground to cover. Keep in mind that growing into what God has created us to be—whether we are men or women—is an ongoing process. We walk by faith, clinging to His grace every step of the way. I hope you will consider the following chapters as guideposts to help you on your journey, that what I share will help you to reconcile your thinking in troublesome areas. I pray it will give you a new outlook on your God-ordained identity as well as on the state of your relationships with women.

This book is also for women, single and married. Did you know that your posture toward the men in your lives can dramatically affect the outcome of your relationships? Single or married, we first need to make sure our expectations of our men are aligned with God's Word. Second, we need to understand the contribution we can make to nurturing God's possibilities and helping them become reality in our man's life. Women do have an important part to play in completing a man and helping him become all that God created and designed him to be.

Singles, I hope to give you guidelines on what to look for in a man and how to recognize God's man for you. If you go shopping for diamonds without any knowledge of what to look for, any diamond will look good. Once you've been educated, however, you will make more careful choices. Discerning buyers know what to look for in the clarity, color, cut, and carat weight. They know what they won't settle for. They also know the true value of the stone and whether it matches the price tag. Love and marriage are a jewel in the making. You've got to start with the right stone, however, in order to emerge with anything of lasting value.

Wives, I hope to give you a clear view of what God wants your husband to be and how you can be instrumental in nurturing those character traits in your man. To take the diamond metaphor a step further, it is possible to have the right stone, apply the wrong pressure, and end up with a worthless rock. I hope to help you avoid this pitfall.

For those of you who feel you married a worthless rock, just remember that all you need is the right jeweler. Under the careful hand of the Master Cutter, that rock can take on a brilliance you didn't know was possible. Proverbs 27:17 says, "As iron sharpens iron, so one man [or woman] sharpens another." Perhaps in this word picture we should say that a man and a woman can polish each other until they both shine as brilliantly as God intended. So don't get frustrated; the possibilities are endless.

Men, you might be tempted to have the same reaction to the Proverbs 31 man as women do to the Proverbs 31 woman. Again, keep in mind that we are all works in progress. How long it takes you to complete the journey does not matter, but your commitment to continue moving onward and upward does.

It is my prayer that men and women alike will be liberated in their thinking, inspired in their spirit, and spurred on by a new hope for the future of their relationships with members of the opposite sex. I hope we all will become aware of our responsibilities in forging strong relationships and willing to give and take as we submit our natural longings to the Word of God. May the blessings that come from being a man or woman after God's own heart pleasantly surprise us all.

RECOGNIZING THE VOICE

Knowing Your God

The LORD would speak to Moses face to face,
as a man speaks with his friend.

EXODUS 33:11

The Proverbs 31 man has an intimate knowledge of God.

I personally envy Adam, the first man who walked and talked with God in the Garden of Eden. The account in Genesis tells us that these two enjoyed constant fellowship. Can you imagine the conversations that were held? The insights that God shared with His new creation? The overwhelming sense of well-being that Adam must have felt as God affirmed him as a man, told him of His great love for him, and instructed him in His ways. Adam knew God in a way most of us can only dream of.

Many men know *about* God, but do they really *know* Him? That is the question. Since the Word clearly states that those who believe in and serve God are not to be unequally yoked with unbelievers, it stands to reason that the first qualification for our Proverbs 31 man, if you are a believer, is an intimate relationship with and a personal knowledge of God.

One of the things that garners respect in the heart of a woman—which is a prerequisite to her willingness to submit to her man—is wisdom. A woman needs a man whom she can trust to make wise decisions. Head knowledge alone cannot make a man an effective head of the house as priest and leader. Only a man who is able to seek the rich counsel of the Lord for insight can lead his loved ones wisely. God is the source of that wisdom. The Word promises that those who know their God will be strong and accomplish great things! (See Daniel 11:32.) Wisdom and boldness are birthed out of possessing the confidence that God "has your back."

When I think of men who possess this intimate knowledge of God, several great men of the Bible who made their mark on the world come to mind. These men walked with Him. They talked with Him. They felt His heartbeat and relayed its rhythm to others. They walked in harmony with God's design for their lives. Some made missteps from time to time, but they got back on track and finished their assignments in life.

As we review biblical history, we see men having deep and lengthy conversations with God or even wrestling with Him! These men sought advice, reassurance, and consolation from the one true source of profound and lasting wisdom. "Should I take my family and go to another land, God?" "Which road should I take?" "Should we go to battle now,

Lord?" "Give me the assurance that you will go with us." They did not make major decisions without seeking His face.

INTIMACY THAT TRANSFORMS

Can any man become a Proverbs 31 man? Through Christ all things are possible. Jacob was transformed from a liar and a schemer into a great man by becoming a victim of his own tricks and being broken in spirit and in body. On the day he was able to declare who was *really* Lord of his life, he changed. We'll take a closer look at his life later, but it is interesting to note that his deep love for a woman named Rachel probably had a lot to do with his transformation. Sometimes God uses a woman to complete the change He has begun in the heart of a man. A woman who will not settle for a man "as is"—if she is also submitted to God and not grasping for control—can cause him to grow. The world says that behind every great man is a great woman. This is true. God has placed very specific gifts inside a woman that empower a man to be all that he was created to be. I wrote specifically on these in my book *The Power of Femininity*. Ladies, please feel free to read that book for more specifics on your part in this equation, as I'll be focusing on men in this book.

No man skips the process of transformation except by his own choosing. All must first be broken before becoming a worthy vessel that can please God and gain honor in the eyes of a woman.

Consider Moses. Pampered and living large in Pharaoh's house, he developed the temper of a spoiled child capable of murder. High on Mount Sinai, Moses came face to face with God, and the experience changed him. Standing before the burning bush, set apart from human voices and rationale, Moses dared to ask the mighty God who He was. How God longs to hear that question from the lips of every one of His creations! How willing He is to answer. Yes, Moses beheld God in His awesomeness. Moses was also humbled in His presence. The holy presence of God exposed him. All that he was and was not suddenly became clearly evident. Moses stood in the light of truth and had to respond. With all pretense and defenses laid aside, nothing could stand between this all-powerful, infinite God and this man who had finally made peace with his own finiteness. In this place, Moses came to know God intimately, which made them partners—one in mind and spirit. Moses came back down that mountain a different man, his soul bursting with divine purpose. He had an assignment from God—the deliverance of Israel—and was determined to complete it. This same man who had impulsively killed an Egyptian became a man who searched God's heart in every decision he made concerning the nation of Israel.

No one is perfect, not even a Proverbs 31 man. No one walks in the Spirit continuously. Even Moses was given to impatience when leading his whining charges toward the Promised Land. Because his heart was tender toward God, however, Moses was quick to repent and gracefully get back on track. This is another central trait in the man we seek: He bears the consequences of his mistakes, takes a licking, and keeps on ticking. His spirit is not bowed or crushed by adversity, and he doesn't blame others for his problems. He simply takes responsibility and finds a solution. He allows perseverance to finish its work in him so he "may be mature and complete, not lacking anything" (James 1:4).

This maturity makes him a solid rock on which his family can stand. They are secure because he has anchored himself in God alone. He earns their trust through endurance and consistency. Moses could take the heat. He stood before Pharaoh without flinching and demanded that this powerful monarch let God's people go. He was able to confront the enemy and stand his ground because he had the full assurance that God stood with him. He understood that it was not by might, not by power, but by the Spirit of God about and within him that he would be able to accomplish a mission that seemed impossible.

> *Women need men who will seek God's face and secure their future by obedience to His instructions.*

FOLLOW THAT MAN!

Oh, the world needs more men who are willing to be transformed by God and plugged into His wisdom! Time and again men such as Abraham, Jacob, Moses, and Daniel made decisions based on the counsel they received from on high and were blessed mightily as a result. Whenever they charged ahead in their own strength, making decisions based on the flesh and not in the Spirit, they floundered and failed miserably. Is it any wonder God grieved when Adam followed Eve's lead and ate the forbidden fruit? The consequences of such impulses affect the lives of families, communities, nations, and even the world. Today we all bear the effects of Adam's sin.

Women need men who will seek God's face and secure their future by obedience to His instructions. God told Abraham to take his family and go to a place He would reveal later. Can you imagine? How ready would the average woman be to drop everything—her home, her friends, her career, her kids' education—if her husband came home and said, "Baby, the Lord said that we should move, so get packed and let's go."

"Oh? Well, where are we going?"

"I don't know. He hasn't told me yet, but I thought we would just start driving and find out." I don't think that would go over well *unless* that man had a sound record of hearing correctly from God.

Perhaps Lot's wife looked back at Sodom even after the angels had instructed them not to because she doubted her husband's decision to leave their home (see Genesis 19:17,26). Though they lived in affluence, Lot was an impulsive type who typically made decisions from his head. This was the same man who chose to remove himself from the safe leadership of Abraham and relocate his family to the center of an atrociously godless society (13:10-13). This same man offered his own daughters to rowdy, lecherous men in exchange for the well-being of two strangers he didn't even know (19:8). How could his wife completely trust his choice at this juncture? He didn't even exude confidence himself regarding the angels' instructions (19:18-19)! Could this be yet another bad decision that would cost them everything? It's safe to guess that Lot's wife had doubts as she fled her comfortable life.

Though humans hold one another to a tougher standard of perfection, God is gracious to have mercy on us when we mess up. Adam's sin, precipitated by Eve, is considered by most scholars to be a premeditated, blatant act of disobedience. Yet God reestablished him, covered him, and gave him a second chance at life.

Even Abraham missed it from time to time, but he got it right often enough that his wife, Sarah—first called Sarai—gave him her confidence. Let's take a look at the time Abraham—then called Abram—passed through Egypt, and word reached the Pharaoh that Abraham was traveling in the company of a very beautiful woman (see Genesis 12:11-20). Abraham, fearing for the lives of all his entourage, encouraged Sarah to say she was his sister. Sarah didn't put her hands on her hips and say, "Now, why would I do a thing like that?" She submitted to his instructions and soon found herself put up at Pharaoh's palace. It took the intervention of God to get them all out of the situation.

This same scenario did not happen once but *twice* as they made their way to the land that God had promised to them (see Genesis 20:2). Why, even after knowing that claiming to be Abraham's sister was not the right thing to do, did Sarah trust Abraham with her life? Some might argue that she obeyed for cultural reasons, but let's face it: Even then feisty women had ways of getting around their husbands' will, but Sarah followed his instructions without protesting. Why? I believe she did because Abraham had a record of following God. Most of the decisions he had made were right-on, and his family had been mightily blessed by his obedience. Sarah trusted God above Abraham to keep her out of harm's way, and indeed, He was faithful. She mastered the art of submitting to her husband as unto the Lord, who was the ultimate authority in both of their lives.

> One of the most beautiful things I ever heard a wife say about her husband was: "It feels as if God is loving me through my husband. It's almost as if he anticipates my needs and meets them before I even say a word." Only a man who prays and hears from God can do such a thing for his wife.

Abraham accumulated great wealth and became well known in the land. His faith brought about the child that had been promised to him and Sarah (see Hebrews 11:11). Now, of course, I must point out what happens to this same man when a woman's influence causes him to abandon his God-given instincts. God will hold him personally responsible for any and all decisions he makes. It is already in the nature of a man, no matter how godly, to try to figure things out in his own mind when things aren't going according to his schedule. Enter woman, in the form of Sarah, stage left. She suggests Abraham sleep with their maid Hagar in order to get the promised child, and Abraham agrees without consulting God (see Genesis 16:2). The union does indeed yield a child, Ishmael, but he is not the one God was talking about, and we've had worldwide problems ever since.

It is obvious that the virtuous woman of Proverbs 31 yielded to the leadership of her husband because he knew and followed the leading of God. Then, unlike Sarah, she sifted her own wisdom and intuitive gifts through the instruction of the Lord before making any suggestions. Proverbs 31:26 says that she speaks with wisdom and faithful instruction is on her tongue. "Faithful to whom?" you might ask. Faithful to the leadership of the Lord and her husband. Ladies, if you want a Proverbs 31 man, you've got to be a Proverbs 31 woman. Men, you need to look past the pretty face of a woman and carefully consider her character before selecting her for your wife.

After having her own son, Isaac, Sara demanded that Hagar and Ishmael be sent away. Though it grieved Abraham to part with a child who was a part of him, he followed the instructions of the Lord to maintain peace and focus on rearing his promised child (see Genesis 21:11-12). A Proverbs 31 man will make such sacrifices for the sake of his wife and household, though they might cause him personal pain. He follows the leading of the Lord at all costs, and if he must abandon something of value, he trusts God's sovereign ability to restore it. He takes his position of leadership seriously and counts the cost of his decisions before making a move. God promised to bless and prosper Ishmael, thereby comforting Abraham and easing the pain of his mistake (21:13).

THE POWER OF A PRAYING MAN

Several years ago I worked for my cousin, who was a bishop from Africa. He was a great man of prayer who spent hours in the presence of God daily. I knew he had God's ear. When I had a need, I was quick to ask him to pray for me. When we traveled, sometimes upsetting circumstances would arise, but I always knew things would work out because I was with a man who was securely connected to God. I felt safe. His life changed mine. His devoted example convicted me to pursue a deeper prayer life myself. As I did, I found my level of faith rising, because I was experiencing true intimacy with God. I felt linked to Him.

The Proverbs 31 man knows his God because he is a man of prayer. His prayer life affects the security of his loved ones.

Let me give you the backdrop of one of my favorite portions of Scripture. On the cusp of entering the Promised Land, Moses sends his spies to check it out before invading. The men come back with an evil report: There are giants in the land. The Israelites cannot possibly go in to occupy it—no way, no how.

God is rather upset with the people's lack of faith and basically regards it as rejection of Him. He asks Moses, "How long will these people treat me with contempt? How long will they refuse to believe in me, in spite of all the miraculous signs I have performed among them? I will strike them down with a plague and destroy them, but I will make you into a nation greater and stronger than they" (Numbers 14:11-12).

The exchange that ensues between God and Moses is profound, illustrating the kind of intimate relationship we are all invited to have with Him. Now, here is the portion of Scripture I love so much:

Moses said to the LORD, "Then the Egyptians will hear about it! By your power you brought these people up from among them. And they will tell the inhabitants of this land about it. They have already heard that you, O LORD, are with these people and that you, O LORD, have been seen face to face, that your cloud stays over them, and that you go before them in a pillar of cloud by day and a pillar of fire by night. If you put these people to death all at one time, the nations who have heard this report about you will say, 'The LORD was not able to bring these people into the land he promised them on oath; so he slaughtered them in the desert.'

"Now may the Lord's strength be displayed, just as you have declared: 'The LORD is slow to anger, abounding in love and forgiving sin and rebellion. Yet he does not leave the guilty unpunished; he punishes the children for the sin of the fathers to the third and fourth generation.' In accordance with your great love, forgive the sin of these people, just as you have pardoned them from the time they left Egypt until now."

The LORD replied, "I have forgiven them, as you asked." (Numbers 14:13-20)

Another translation says that God said He would do what Moses asked because he was His friend! They had a unique friendship. That God would share His emotions and His heart with a man, listen to his response, and consider his words is incredible. They had a two-way conversation; Moses spoke and God answered! As a matter of fact, God *did what Moses requested!* This is the influence that can only be wielded in a secure relationship. Oh for men who can bend the ear of God and get results not only for themselves but also for their wives and loved ones, for their communities and nations!

A praying man is a powerful man. A man who touches the heart of God is desirable to a woman. His relationship with God is evident in the sensitivity he exhibits toward her. The sense of protection she feels under his prayerful care cannot be articulated.

Only through prayer will a man fully know how to meet his wife's needs. She will never be able to vocalize all that she needs from him, and at times, she herself will not even know her own needs. But through his interaction with God and instruction from the Holy Spirit, he will be equipped to respond to the secret desires of her heart. This will not occur if he merely goes through the motions and prays formularized monologues. Real prayer involves a transparency of the heart and an openness to God's response.

How does God respond? Sometimes He responds Spirit to spirit; you just have a deep sense of knowing the answer to your heartfelt questions. He also speaks through His written Word. As you turn the pages, a scripture will come alive to you, speaking the answer you seek. He speaks through others. In our conversations and interaction with them, a word, an encouragement, or an answer is given that settles the issues of our hearts. Sometimes God speaks to us in our dreams. God speaks in many ways, but He definitely seeks to speak to His men. He also seeks men who will respond to His words, blessing their families as well as others.

One of the most beautiful things I ever heard a wife say about her husband was: "It feels as if God is loving me through my husband. He is so sensitive to my needs. It's almost as if he anticipates them and meets them before I even say a word." Only a man who prays and hears from God can do such a thing for his wife.

Of course, prayer doesn't just affect a man's relationship with his wife and her perception of him. It affects his standing in the workplace.

The time a man spends in prayer, worshiping God and consulting His wisdom, is a time of gathering priceless insight that equips him to be excellent in the marketplace. Since the Proverbs 31 woman's husband was well thought of in the gates (verse 23), we can conclude he had a significant amount of integrity, wisdom, and success at work; after all, these are the character traits that men admire in other men. These are also evidence of a man who follows after God and heeds His direction.

Daniel, whose story is told in the book of Daniel, is a great example of this. He was known in the king's court as a man of prayer and extreme wisdom. Here was a religious man who survived four administrations of ungodly leaders! His gift of wisdom made room for him, so much so that the fourth king intended to promote him to be vice-king, in a sense (see Daniel 6:3).

The other underlings became jealous and plotted his demise. When they could find no dirt to smear Daniel's character and ruin him, they manipulated the king into making a decree that would require Daniel to stop praying, which they knew he would not do. They set Daniel up for a fall they knew he would take. The king was not a happy camper when he found out that he'd have to put his favorite worker to death, but he could not go back on his word. Into the lions' den Daniel must go (see 6:4-16).

The extraordinary turn of events that took place after that is a clear testimony to the power of a praying man. This heathen king was so grieved over losing Daniel that he himself resorted to fasting and prayer on Daniel's behalf! First thing in the morning he went to check the condition of his favorite charge and found Daniel still alive. God had sent angels to shut the lions' mouths. So impressed was he with the power of God that he ordered his devious employees who had concocted this scheme to be thrown into the lions' den to their death.

Then he proclaimed that everyone throughout the land should worship Daniel's God (see 6:25-28). Talk about being spoken well of in the gates! Daniel's story is the epitome of how this could come about.

Many women reading this account right now are saying to themselves, "Well, where are these praying men?" Or, "My husband does not pray as he should. How can I get him to pray like that? I feel as if I am carrying the entire prayer load in my family." My suggestion is a simple one. Continue in prayer yourself, asking God to make your mate a man of prayer. Learn about God for yourself by studying your Bible to find out more about Him. Ask Him to reveal to you His personality and character—how He thinks, feels, and operates. The more you know about Him, the more intimate your relationship with Him will be, because your prayer life will change. When you understand His heart, you can have true conversations with Him. The things you learn will stir up your passion and excitement. The result? That same excitement and passion will become contagious. More than likely, your husband will feel compelled to learn more and to have his own incredible experiences with God that he can share with you. Make sure that you share with your partner as an equal and do not lecture him as if he is a lesser pupil.

Take the initiative to ask your husband to pray for you and with you. Don't give him a daily lecture about his need to pray. Let him know of the need you have to feel covered by him with his prayers. Encourage him to see the answers to his prayers. This will make him feel empowered, and he will take over the reins on his own as he begins to see the difference that prayer makes in his life and your world collectively.

Single women can be praying even now for a prayerful man who knows his God.

There are many dimensions of a man that must be developed in order for him to become the extraordinary man whom every woman seeks and whom God smiles upon. He is a work in progress. As we continue to study the different aspects of the character traits that make a man a king among men, remember that the foundation of all growth is his relationship with God. This one thing alone will give him the ability to walk in both the spiritual as well as the natural world and to make wise choices based on his knowledge of both.

Men, if the idea of seeking a deeper prayer life and a richer relationship with God overwhelms you, allow me to offer a few simple suggestions. First of all, do not set a high, lofty goal for yourself. This usually shuts us down before we even begin. Commit to reserving a specific period of time to the Lord daily, even if it is only five minutes. Trust me, you will find yourself staying longer in His presence once you get started. Write down the concerns that weigh heavy on your heart, and discuss them with your Lord. Select a devotional that will help jumpstart your conversation with God. Two that I highly recommend are *My Utmost for His Highest* by Oswald Chambers and *Day by Day* by Kevin Boa. Both are short and sweet but profound, definitely rich with food for thought. Select a scripture to meditate on throughout the day or week, and ask God to give you a thorough understanding of it.

Intentionally, deliberately *choose* to spend time with God until it becomes a habit. God will do the rest of the work. You will find your friendship with God deepening into something you find you do not care to live without. The wisdom of God is indispensable when wrestling with the seen and the unseen components of everyday living. Victory comes not from fighting with physical muscle but from falling on bended knees in submission to God and love for Him.

If you are not yet convinced of the power of a man's prayers, let me leave you with this, and allow it to speak for itself. "Isaac prayed to the LORD on behalf of his wife, because she was barren. The LORD answered his prayer, and his wife Rebekah became pregnant" (Genesis 25:21). And again I say, truly a woman needs a man who can pray.

————

The man without the Spirit does not accept the things
that come from the Spirit of God, for they are
foolishness to him, and he cannot understand them,
because they are spiritually discerned.

1 CORINTHIANS 2:14

The Proverbs 31 man knows God intimately; therefore, he is able to discern the needs of the woman in his life.

FOR REFLECTION AND DISCUSSION

For Him

"Although a wicked man commits a hundred crimes and still lives a long time, I know that it will go better with God-fearing men, who are reverent before God" (Ecclesiastes 8:12). The man who has an intimate knowledge of the heart and mind of God is consistent in garnering victories in his life, no matter how many trials and tests he faces. Prayer and the wisdom gained from it make him stand heads above his peers.

- How is your relationship with God?
- What is your attitude toward prayer? What would make you take the time to pray more?
- What type of input do you need from God in order to be victorious in your life? Recall a time when a solution came to you as a result of prayer?
- What sources do you seek for wisdom? Is God on that list?
- After exhausting your own resources of reason, where do you turn?

For Her

"Charm is deceptive, and beauty is fleeting; but a woman who fears the LORD is to be praised" (Proverbs 31:30). The one lasting quality a woman can possess is, without fail, wisdom. The wise woman makes choices that make the heart of a man stay with her. Though you should never neglect your physical appearance, don't rely solely on outward beauty. The internal will keep you beautiful in your man's eyes.

- How is your relationship with God?
- Are you in the habit of regularly seeking His face for wisdom, or do you move impulsively based on your own reasoning?
- How would you describe your prayer life? What keeps it from being better? How can you change this?
- Do others regard you as a woman of prayer? How is that evident in your life?
- What are you doing to encourage the man in your life to be prayerful? Are you requiring him or inspiring him to pray?

For You Both

The couple that prays together reaches levels of intimacy that bond them together as true partners facing the challenges of life.

- When would be the perfect time for you to have joint devotions and discuss the issues on your heart? Are you willing to set aside the time? What boundaries will you have to set to make this happen?
- How can you encourage each other to be more prayerful?
- What hinders you from having the type of prayer life that you desire? What can you do to support each other in improving this area?
- How much time do you spend in the Word? Are you able to apply what you read to your life and relationships? In what areas do you have difficulty? What could help you to practically apply biblical principles to your everyday life? How does this make you more sensitive to your partner's needs?
- How can you better share the heart of God with your spouse as your relationship with the Lord deepens?

2

YOU'VE GOT POTENTIAL

Pursuing Your Purpose

For God does speak—now one way, now another—though man
may not perceive it. In a dream, in a vision of the night,
when deep sleep falls on men as they slumber in their beds.

JOB 33:14-15

The Proverbs 31 man has a vision for his life
and a secure sense of purpose and destiny.

The man without a sense of purpose is like a piece of driftwood float-
ing aimlessly down a river. It picks up everything in its path, becoming
sodden and weighted with debris, until it finally decays and falls apart.
This is what purposelessness does to a soul.

When women who have accomplished much encounter men who
are intimidated by their endeavors, they want to know why. To a
certain extent, women may be to blame: Their behavior sometimes

suggests they are completely self-reliant and don't need or want a man, even if they do. It is difficult for most men to embrace the fact that a woman's first desire is to be loved, regardless of her worldly success. But a careful consideration of the question reveals a more profound answer: Those who have not yet discovered their purpose in many cases feel they have nothing to offer those who have.

It is important for a man to have a sense of purpose. In his book *Wild at Heart*, John Eldridge says that every man has to have an adventure to live, a battle to fight, and a beauty to rescue. A woman needs an adventure to share in, to be fought for, and to have her beauty acknowledged. Sometimes the battle is within, sometimes without. Regardless, a man must fight and win his own personal wars. This real need is a God-given desire. God wants everyone to end his or her day with a sense of fulfillment and satisfaction. The day was spent laboring, yes, but purposefully, in tandem with God's call.

> *A strong man, however, knows that a strong woman does not diminish him or God's call on his life. Instead, she can actually give him the inspiration he needs to locate and reach his goal.*

What made the Proverbs 31 man so secure that he could release his wife to be the thriving entrepreneur that she was? I believe he was secure in his own mission and identity. A Proverbs 31 man has a great sense of well-being because he feels fulfilled in his own work and accomplishments; therefore, he is able to celebrate the strengths of others, including those of his wife. He in turn will serve her and encourage her in her endeavors.

On the other hand, those who simply work to eke out an existence are irritated by those who come alive in the course of their responsibilities. It is difficult to celebrate others when you cannot celebrate yourself. A man without a sense of purpose can destroy even the best of relationships. Devoid of personal fulfillment, he will be incapable of serving his wife—or anyone else—as he should. Should she make any strides toward fulfilling her own personal vision, he will block her path, fearing that she will surpass him. For a man harboring self-doubt, an accomplished woman might raise the bar on his life. If he feels helpless to clear the bar or chooses to resist the work it takes, he will flee from the relationship rather than pursue it.

A strong man, however, knows that a strong woman does not diminish him or God's call on his life. Instead, she can actually give him the inspiration he needs to locate and reach his goal.

WHERE PURPOSE MEETS PASSION

The marketplace is flooded with literature on how to lead a life full of purpose. Christians in particular believe that all men and women are here for a specific purpose, though we each have individual assignments that align with our innate gifts and talents. Well, what if you don't know your purpose? What if you don't know what your gifts are? Then it is time to revisit what you are passionate about and unite that passion with your natural abilities.

Martin Luther King Jr. was a natural speaker. He had a way with words that inspired and motivated others. This natural ability, coupled with his passion for the plight of people being treated unjustly, formed the platform for a crusade that liberated a people.

Some say you cannot make money by doing what you like or by doing what comes naturally to you. However, it is quite possible if you find the right outlet for your inherent giftings. Your God-given purpose will always coincide with someone's need. You will always be excellent at what you are passionate about. People are always willing to pay for what they need if it is truly excellent.

I always loved to write as a child, but I never saw writing as a way to make a living in later years. I studied commercial art and advertising and had a wonderful career that reaped many awards, yet I was not satisfied. Though my career brought excitement, my greatest pleasure still came from quiet moments of writing. I also had an intense love for the Word of God. I was passionate about the fact that I wanted Christians to see the practical advice God had to offer on any given subject, but especially relationships.

Years later, after accepting a challenge from my mentor, P. B. Wilson, to write about the revelations that God was giving me and the victories I was experiencing as a single woman, the purpose for my life became apparent. God blessed my writing and changed my life, my career, my everything! Not only did it put me in the position to prosper beyond what I had experienced in my first career, but it allowed me to exercise my passion to the fullest by sharing the truth of God's Word with others through several different mediums. I felt that I was finally making God smile as well as blessing the lives of others. The feeling of fulfillment is beyond what I could have imagined. I know that I am in the center of God's divine plan for my life.

> *We all have been given dreams. Making them come to life is where the dragon-slaying and damsel-saving adventure begins.*

At the same time, fulfilling our God-given purpose does not necessarily mean we will be financially successful. Sometimes the people in need are not able to pay with money, even if they are willing. But God is able to take care of those whose service is rooted in obedience to Him rather than in the pursuit of material compensation. The riches of personal fulfillment easily compensate for the lack of material reward when one is living a life of purpose. Mother Teresa spent years serving the impoverished of India and said she felt richer than those who possessed much wealth. In contrast, wealth was an obstacle for the rich young ruler who encountered Jesus. He was unwilling to release his riches to embrace his purpose. He went on his way financially wealthy but spiritually and emotionally bankrupt—a sad prisoner of his many possessions (see Matthew 19:16-22).

Joseph—you know, the one with the multicolored coat—was passionate about pleasing his father. Are you passionate about pleasing your heavenly Father? Joseph was obedient to his father. He did what his father asked of him. His father asked him to check on his brothers, take them provisions, and bring back a report of their well-being (see Genesis 37:14). Our heavenly Father asks the same thing of us: to seek the welfare of those around us and serve where possible so that a good report can be made on the condition of the human race.

How does a man find his purpose? The search begins with a man examining his heart and returning to the seat of his passion. Women can be instrumental in this process, discussing and discovering areas of interest and giving encouragement.

In his book *The Assignment,* famed wisdom teacher Mike Murdoch says to ask yourself the following questions: What makes you angry? What makes you so grieved that you cannot stop talking about it? What sparks your interest? What makes you come alive in conversation or debate? The answers to these questions probably hold the clue to the puzzle you were created to solve. Martin Luther King Jr. was not the only man to have a dream. We all have been given dreams. Making them come to life is where the dragon-slaying and damsel-saving adventure begins.

Sometimes in our pursuit of a dream or doing something that we enjoy, life happens. For some people, the unexpected becomes a stepping-stone to bigger and better things. For others, it becomes a detour that leads to a place where life seems easier and more practical, but certainly not as joyful. These people are haunted by their original dream but have lost sight of how to achieve it. They settle into a generic existence where the only reminder that they are not what, or where, they should be is an encounter with someone who is. Their response in such an encounter can be either to take a deep breath and get back on track or flee from the person who reminds them of the dream they've lost.

Every adventure has twists and turns. Every good movie has a kink in the plot that forces the hero to make a hard decision. Does he let the object of his desire get away or does he fight for it? At this point a woman sometimes enters the story to help him drive the getaway car, get kidnapped so he has to rescue her, or build his confidence so he can accomplish his mission. But sometimes that man must walk alone, fueled by his own determination to complete what he began.

THE LEADER IN EVERY MAN

Joseph in the book of Genesis was such a man. A lone dreamer. He had no idea how his dream would come to pass, but it birthed a sense of purpose in his life that no trial could deter. Joseph had a dream. A dream that he would rise to greatness. Not every man is going to be a renowned ruler of a powerful land. Every man was created, however, to be a great ruler—over his home, his work environment, his church, or

his community. He was created to be a great leader of people. An origi-
nator of causes. An establisher of order, precedents, and ideals.

God gave the original man, Adam, complete charge over His creation. God created Eve to help Adam carry out God's instructions to subdue the earth and keep things in order
(see Genesis 1:28). This same assignment
is built into the spirit of every man, but
it has been crushed on many levels. In
today's equal-opportunity culture, leader-

> *The innate desire to lead
> should never be squelched
> in any man. It should be
> celebrated and refined.*

ship abilities in men are often defined as macho or arrogant, giving
these natural instincts and gifts a negative connotation. It must be
understood that machismo and arrogance are not leadership qualities; they are character flaws that are usually rooted in insecurity or
immaturity.

For those who want to be the leaders God has created them to be,
resistance to that leadership can be withering. When a man comes up
against this attitude from a woman, he may choose to resign, abdicate
his post, and go in search of another venue where he can be true to who
he is. It is true that ungodly leadership can turn to tyranny if not tem-
pered, but the innate desire to lead should never be squelched in any
man. It should be celebrated and refined. Women, encourage the good
of what your man does, and gently speak the truth in love about the
areas that are rough and untempered, but never stifle his spirit. A man
must have an outlet to manifest what was placed in his spirit from the
beginning.

More often than not, in a man's efforts to become a leader, cultivating a heart that is willing to serve is overlooked. This may be one
reason why a man's desire to lead is criticized. But true leadership
requires a man to develop the heart of a servant. One cannot lead

effectively if he does not know how to serve. In this regard, Joseph was a stellar example (see Genesis 39). Sold into slavery far from his home, Joseph found himself in Egypt in a place beneath his station in life. But in the house of Potiphar, Joseph was humbled and learned to serve. In serving, compassion for his fellowman and integrity were birthed. May I dare say that self-control and tact also developed in this place where Joseph could not freely speak his mind. Beyond that, he learned practical skills, nurtured administrative gifts, and gained a knowledge of this foreign people and their customs and language. All of these things would be useful in facilitating his dream when it came to light.

So the first step to becoming a leader is to understand that there is honor in being a servant. I believe there was a day that is not recorded in the Bible when Joseph finally surrendered to God's will and decided to be the best he could be in his immediate assignment. This was the defining moment that turned the tide for Joseph and propelled him toward his destiny. The last vestiges of what he felt entitled to melted away, and he purposed in his heart to serve wholeheartedly and count it a privilege to do so.

Long before this, however, Joseph decided to share his dream with loved ones, and he met with very real resentment. His brothers scoffed at him and said,

"Do you intend to reign over us? Will you actually rule us?" And they hated him all the more because of his dream and what he had said.

Then he had another dream, and he told it to his brothers. "Listen," he said, "I had another dream, and this time the sun and moon and eleven stars were bowing down to me."

When he told his father as well as his brothers, his father rebuked him and said, "What is this dream you had? Will your mother and I and your brothers actually come and bow down to the ground before you?" (Genesis 37:8-10)

This could have been very discouraging, but Joseph did not abandon his vision. It burned in his heart. The flame was not put out even when his brothers sold him into slavery. Sometimes the jealousy of others can put you in bondage. It can break your spirit and make you discard your dreams, but remember: Life is an adventure. Though the plot may thicken, one must persevere. The higher the calling, the more warfare there will be against it. Someone once said, "Higher levels mean you have bigger devils to fight." The greatest victories in life come after a tremendous fight, disappointment, or setback. And fight to the finish you must—past the naysaying of others and past the restraints they might try to place on your mind. You must hold on to the original vision.

FOCUSED FORWARD

There was no easy path or shortcut to the fulfillment of Joseph's dreams, though they were presented to him. Shortcuts usually lead to dead ends, and he had the wisdom to stay away from those. Joseph knew a tryst with the boss's wife was not the route to take, though everyone does not appreciate those who take the upright path (see Genesis 39:7-20). You must press past invitations that take you off your course. Have you ever noticed when on a diet that everyone keeps offering you all the wrong things to eat? They can't bear to eat alone! It takes everything within you to stay on your mission.

To stay on your course, you must hold fast to your vision, the revelation of why you are here and where you are going. "Where there is no revelation [or vision], the people cast off restraint; but blessed is he who keeps the law" (Proverbs 29:18). The man with a plan will not compromise. He will stay focused on the path set before him. He will stick to the law that rules his heart and decisions. The man who is focused will sometimes appear to be ruthless, but actually he is simply determined to reach his destination. He knows that he will be of greater benefit to others if he can fill the position he was created for.

As you hold fast, I urge you to adhere to godly counsel. In the strength of your determination, be sure not to slip into selfishness and overlook the needs of others. Instead, persevere in faith as you are led by the Holy Spirit to reach your breakthrough and embrace your goal. Submit to the training of life, knowing that every experience, even the negative ones, are preparing you for the path that you will ultimately take (see James 1:2-4). Accumulate the wisdom afforded even in the places that feel like delays and detours. With God on your side and an intimate relationship with Him, you will eventually reach your destination.

When I think of such focused commitment I think again of Daniel. Captive in Babylon, his loss of freedom did not deter him from his sense of purpose. He refused to eat the king's bread and sumptuous foods or to defile himself in any way, knowing that opulence would give way to distraction. Daniel needed to hear God's voice and have a clear direction for his life even in a place where his captors put limitations on him (see Daniel 1:17-20). In the end, Daniel's wisdom surpassed everyone's in the court (see Daniel 2:48-49). He was able to read the handwriting on the wall when no one else could and give wise counsel and godly instruction as to its meaning to the benefit of all (see Daniel 5). He stayed focused and fulfilled the divine call on his life.

A man with a divine sense of purpose does not make excuses for not moving forward. Though Joseph landed in jail after Potiphar's wife falsely accused him of rape, he never lost sight of his dream. For him, each step took him closer to the fulfillment of God's original intention, although he had no way of knowing how he would get there. But in the right time, the moment came for him to be unleashed into his destiny, and he was ready. Being ready is crucial to the fulfillment of a dream. Preparation and opportunity must meet in order for success to be birthed. There is no such thing as waiting for the lucky break and then gathering all of your ducks to put them in a row. Consistency in nurturing your dream must begin with you. Proverbs 24:27 says, "Finish your outdoor work and get your fields ready; after that, build your house." In other words, do what is necessary to secure your home—the place where you live, the center of your life. The focused man who knows his purpose makes his career goals work around his personal goals. When the two are in harmony, he will have a clear image of where he is going and how he needs to get there. Also, his preparation will make provision for the life he wants to build for himself and his family.

> *A Proverbs 31 man will receive his assignment in life before receiving his wife. This is God's perfect order for a man's life: assignment first, helper second.*

ASSIGNMENT FIRST, HELPER SECOND

After many years of being confined to jail, Joseph got his day before Pharaoh and was promoted to his right-hand man. Pharaoh also rewarded Joseph with a wife because of Joseph's faithful service to him. A Proverbs 31 man will receive his assignment in life before receiving his wife. This is God's perfect order for a man's life. A man cannot choose the right partner if he doesn't know what his job description for life is! Eve was created to be a helpmeet for Adam. Adam needed a partner who came equipped with everything he needed in order to carry out the charge he had been given. After Jacob received a wife, he grew into a true leader. Though some had wives before getting their call later in life—such as Noah and Abraham—their wives were obvious partners with them as these men completed their missions.

Singles, this is so important that I'll say it again: You won't know if someone is a good match for you until you know your purpose. Where are you going in life? Your husband or wife will either propel you toward or hold you back from your ultimate destiny. Know your personal job description before "hiring" a partner.

No one hires a person to do a job without knowing if he is capable of fulfilling the job description. Marriage is not just an emotional connection. It's not about garnering just personal satisfaction. Think of it as a business partnership of sorts, in which two people come together for the betterment and empowerment of both to fulfill what God created them to do. Therefore, a man must know where he is going in order to discern whether a woman he meets is walking in the same direction and whether she is gifted and equipped to be a worthy partner.

As a man gains the security that comes with fulfilling his call in life, he can become the catalyst that propels his entire household to embrace their God-given destiny.

A doctor's needs are different from those of an athlete. A minister's needs are different from those of a military officer. The partner a man selects will weigh heavily on how effectively he is able to function in his calling. A woman who is sweet but has no social skills would not make a good politician's wife. She will affect his work as well as the way others view him. The way others view him will affect how she is viewed as well—one influences the other.

From housewife to high-powered executive, each woman needs the same thing—to be loved as a woman and celebrated by her husband for all of her efforts. Just as men seek praise and honor, women crave affirmation from their spouses. Fulfillment of these needs will come as you empower your mate to live up to his or her calling. If you're married and feel you may have put the carriage before the horse, turn to God for wisdom. As you honor the covenant of your marriage and make every effort to support your spouse's vision and endeavors, God can make your partnership work.

THE FREEING POWER OF PURPOSE

Another mysterious behind-the-scenes man was Lappidoth, the husband of Deborah, who was a prophetess and judge over Israel. Now, he had to be a secure man! His wife was running the nation, yet from all accounts he was not a deterrent. Obviously, Lappidoth had it going on in his own right. His name is listed in Scripture. His presence in her life was noted, yet she was a powerhouse as well, as she commanded the army of Israel.

Only a man who is busy with his own dreams and purpose could have the security to release his woman to such a task. A man who is a leader in his own game needs the time and space to do what he does. He welcomes a woman who has things to do. When down time comes, they have a lot to celebrate between the two of them. They can share and exchange victories. The spirit of competition is not present because each of them admires the gifts of the other and draws strength from them.

Many couples are dynamic duos because one partner stays behind the scenes, spurring the other on. That doesn't mean the invisible one has no vision or power, just a different function. Where would a Joyce Meyers be without a Dave? For years I never knew what he looked like, but I knew, via her, that he is an integral part of her success. I know many women who are in the forefront of business and ministry who have husbands that manage them. Together they enjoy the fruits of their labor.

Many men with high profiles attribute their success to their wives. Again, just because we do not see them does not mean they are not a mighty force to be reckoned with. These are intelligent women who feed their husbands words of insight, dress them smartly, and prepare them for battle in the marketplace every day. What do they reap? The bounty of their husband's success. These arrangements only work when both parties understand the breadth of their individual gifts and the specifics of their personal and collective callings as a couple.

In most cases, the partner behind the scenes is the one who wields the most influence in that person's life. Think of Pontius Pilate's wife, who sent a note to her husband cautioning him not to have any part in the crucifixion of Jesus (see Matthew 27:19). We don't know her name, but her little note affected history. For that matter, think of Herodias, who influenced Herod to throw John the Baptist in jail and then later, through the use of her own daughter, got him to behead this mighty prophet of God (see Matthew 14:3-10). This was not a good thing; however, it does say something about the powerful influence of a woman.

Much has been written about the influence of women, positive and negative. But men have the same influence on their wives and their children. As a man gains the security that comes with fulfilling his call in life, he can become the catalyst that propels his entire household to embrace their God-given destiny. His influence and leadership will affect how his daughters view men and how his sons view themselves and their responsibilities.

WHO DOES GOD SAY YOU ARE?

Many men who do not have a firm hold on their purpose in life were raised by purposeless fathers. A lack of significant affirmation in their formative years stunted their growth into manhood and squelched their dreams. Many a parent has earmarked his or her children for far less than they were meant to be. Parents swayed by their own experiences and perceptions of their children often subconsciously or consciously urge their children to settle for far less than their true purpose in life.

It's good to know that "man looks at the outward appearance, but the LORD looks at the heart" (1 Samuel 16:7). Women should be careful not to consider only the outward appearance of a man; they should take a deeper look at his heart. God is the rebuilder of men! He delights in finding those who view themselves as insignificant and raising them up to be mighty warriors. Men like David, king

> *God delights in finding men who view themselves as insignificant and raising them up to be mighty warriors.*

of Israel. When Samuel the prophet took a trip to Jesse's house intending to crown one of his sons as king, Jesse gathered his oldest sons and awaited Samuel's verdict. He never even bothered to call David home. David? King? Impossible! But Samuel, full of the Spirit of God, asked

Jesse if these seven sons were all that he had. Jesse replied that the youngest one was tending sheep (see 1 Samuel 16:6-13).

Can you imagine how shocked the entire family was when David was anointed to be the next king of Israel? Sometimes a man needs someone to whisper in his ear that he is a king. *King!* Those words can start a fire in his heart that will consume him with passion to live up to his calling. But in so doing, a man has to be able to cast down the names he has been called by man and respond to the name that he is called by God.

Poor Gideon, whose story is told in the book of Judges, had an insecurity complex that was probably birthed from listening to his father and those in his clan. They saw themselves as insignificant and powerless. When God approached Gideon about leading Israel against their enemy the Midianites, He called Gideon a mighty man of valor! Gideon could not accept the title. He rattled off all the excuses for failure he had ever heard. "'But Lord,' Gideon asked, 'how can I save Israel? My clan is the weakest in Manasseh, and I am the least in my family'" (Judges 6:15). Where did that come from? Do you think he just came up with that on his own? Who had told him he was the least in his family? If it is true that what a man thinks reveals what he is, Gideon was in deep trouble.

Our thoughts become our beliefs. We act on our beliefs. If you believe you are nothing, then you will *be* nothing because you will *do* nothing to change your situation. Why? Because you believe you deserve to be where you are, and you expect nothing more. However, God will never let someone whom He has called for a specific purpose settle for less than that. Every man will have a day of reckoning, be it woman or circumstance, that will shake him at the very core of his being and say, "Wake up! Smell the coffee and get busy!" Some will go back to sleep and spend a lifetime bemoaning a meaningless existence. Others will grab the challenge by the horns and rise to new levels of courage and accomplishment.

Gideon asked God for confirmation after confirmation before he rose to the occasion and led Israel to victory. A man who understands the limitations of his humanness—his finiteness—also understands why his relationship with God and his choice of a woman are crucial to his success. With a spirit that is sensitive to God's instruction for his life, as well as the right woman by his side feeding him constant reassurance, he can surpass his wildest dreams and experience a great sense of accomplishment.

A woman is called to replace the lies of the enemy in her man's life with the truth of God's Word: With Christ, all things are possible. Remember that Eve was able to get Adam to partake of the fruit he knew he shouldn't eat. Be cognizant of the fact that whatever a woman feeds a man, whether food for his soul or seeds of destructive thinking, he will internalize it, and that woman will live with the fruit of her own handiwork. It takes a strong man to stay focused on the Spirit and not heed the words that are like arrows piercing his heart. Few can withstand such assault from a loved one.

Winning the Battle

When Deborah called Barak to inform him that the Lord had commanded that he lead the Israelites into battle, he told her he wouldn't go unless she went with him. She agreed and accompanied him, but not without first telling him that because he refused to go alone, the honor for killing the enemy would go to a woman. When they approached the line of fire, she told him he must go on and fight alone, and Barak obeyed (see Judges 4).

In the heat of the battle, Sisera, the captain of the enemy's army, escaped and made his way to the tent of Jael. After serving him food and milk, she suggested Sisera take a nap. While he was sleeping she drove a tent peg through his brain. The battle was won, and in accordance with Deborah's prophecy, Jael got the accolades for defeating the enemy. Deborah, however, who was called a mother in Israel, displayed a true mother's heart by celebrating Barak's part in the victory. She sang his praises in her celebration song as well as paying tribute to the goodness of the Lord.

What is the point of this illustration? Simply this: In the course of a man's attaining his purpose, there is a time when a woman must be willing to fight with her man. There is a time when a man must let her. There are some things that a woman can do that a man can't and vice versa. God was the first to say man needed help. A real man is able to face his weaknesses and not allow pride to keep him from seeking the help he needs. In the end, it doesn't matter *who* wins the war; it simply must be won. A man needs to choose his battles and know when to call for backup. By focusing on the mission, he cancels out pride. Each partner has a part to play when fighting to achieve a victory in life.

We are quick to examine the wives of politicians who run for office. Why? Because we know after all of the bantering back and forth with their fellow constituents, at the end of the day, what that wife whispers to her husband on their pillow will probably bear more weight than all the debates of the day. Who was it that sang, "Stand by

Your Man"? She had the right idea. Whether it is a career battle or a personal battle, the support of a woman in a man's life can make all the difference in the outcome. For a woman to step away when a man is in his greatest hour of need or decision is to leave him open to the wrong influences or, even worse, to defeat. But to stand and assist or simply say, "I've got your back," has often provided the extra boost many a man has needed to triumph.

Deborah went as far as she could go with Barak, then she pulled back to let him do his thing. She led him to the battle, but she was not going to fight it for him. This is a lesson many women need to learn. A man must be allowed to rise to the occasion. A woman does a tremendous disservice to a man when she enables him to settle for a mediocre existence. She needs to be sensitive to know when to assist and when to release. To allow her man to be "the man." To allow him to feel in charge of his destiny. A man

> *This sense of divine assignment fuels a man and woman to respect each other's gifts and liberates each other to fulfill their individual call, understanding that they will enjoy the benefits corporately.*

would gain more strength than he can imagine by being sensitive enough to know when the touch of a woman will make his way easier and submit to her assistance. Together the war can be won. Now that is a great adventure! To be able to exchange war stories is an incredible way to build intimacy.

TOGETHER ON PURPOSE

Someone asked me recently why so many marriages were crumbling. As we pondered the question, a revelation burst into my spirit. In today's world many are waiting until much later to get married. By then they've often acquired a lot materially and settled into independent lifestyles that are hard to break away from. In years gone by, when couples married younger, they started out with nothing. That young man simply had a dream, and his young bride encouraged him to live it. Together they struggled, bearing between them only a dream for their future together. They built their world together and grew as a family.

There was no "this is mine and that is yours" in their thinking. No "I acquired this and that on my own, so don't get any ideas" attitudes. What they gained together, they shared together, without anyone's trying to hog the credit. They were simply glad they had made it. People stayed together because they had built too much together to destroy it. The stakes were high. Lives had been invested. Blood, sweat, and tears had been spent, and in the end they had something to show for their labor.

In today's world, many men and women have had to fend for themselves, fueled only by their need to make a living and whatever values their parents enforced. The resulting atmosphere has left everyone insecure. Everyone fights for his or her own space, at times knocking the competition, male or female.

Yet God's Word still stands: We were designed with a specific purpose in mind. In the next chapter we'll explore why God designed men and women to work together. The Proverbs 31 man and woman are both purposeful people who are secure, affirmed by God, and empowered with a sense of destiny. It is this sense of divine assignment that fuels them to respect each other's gifts and liberates each other to fulfill their individual call, understanding that they will enjoy the benefits corporately.

It has been said that women major in the minors and men minor in the majors, but the truth of the matter is that men are big-picture people while women are into the details. What a team is made by a man and a woman who understand their differences, value them, and utilize them to each other's advantage, thus creating a beautiful picture of what true love and partnership look like.

———

Blessed are all who fear the LORD, who walk in his ways. You will eat the fruit of your labor; blessings and prosperity will be yours. Your wife will be like a fruitful vine within your house; your sons will be like olive shoots around your table. Thus is the man blessed who fears the LORD.

PSALM 128:1-4

The Proverbs 31 man is a servant leader who regards the achievements of his wife not as competition but as a valuable addition to his own accomplishments.

FOR REFLECTION AND DISCUSSION

For Him

"God blessed them and said to them, 'Be fruitful and increase in number; fill the earth and subdue it. Rule over the fish of the sea and the birds of the air and over every living creature that moves on the ground'" (Genesis 1:28). Every man has received an assignment from God that he must fulfill. This assignment will lead him to a complete life.

- What are you passionate about? What burdens has God laid on your heart? Are you attending to them or ignoring them? If ignoring, why?
- Are you ruled by man's view of you or by God's view of you? Does your view of yourself cause you to compare yourself with others? to your spouse?
- What distractions have you allowed to rob you of your focus?
- What lies has the enemy told you that keep you from being all that you can be? What is God's truth?
- Have you settled for a mediocre existence? If so, why? What will you begin to do differently?

For Her

"The LORD God said, 'It is not good for the man to be alone. I will make a helper suitable for him'" (Genesis 2:18). "She brings him good, not harm, all the days of her life" (Proverbs 31:12). You were created first to worship God and second to assist man in fulfilling his assignment on the earth. Your presence in his life can be the catalyst for failure or success.

- What are you passionate about? Do you know what your personal purpose is? Your purpose in regard to your husband?
- Are you a help or hindrance in his life? How do you facilitate his desire to fulfill his purposes?
- Do you know when to assist and when to release him to fight his own battles?
- How do the opinions of family members and friends affect your view of the man in your life?
- Are you able to see him through God's eyes and embrace the possibilities?

For You Both

An effective partnership is one in which both parties work toward the empowerment and betterment of the other.

- In what ways do you allow each other to settle for a mediocre existence? How do you cause each other to stretch and grow past your comfort zones?
- How do you acknowledge each other's gifts and make positive suggestions that cause each other to put these talents to good use?
- What can you do to help each other visualize the seemingly impossible?
- How can you constructively discuss your dreams and needs with each other? What ground rules will you set to keep each other accountable and transparent in sharing?

3

WHAT'S A RIB BETWEEN FRIENDS?

Embracing Your Design

*The LORD God said, "It is not good for the man to be alone.
I will make a helper suitable for him."*

GENESIS 2:18

A Proverbs 31 man is secure in his manhood.

All right, everyone, it is time to call a truce, lay down our weapons, and let the games begin. Men and women coming together is a good thing. The end, by God. In the previous chapter we began our discussion of Adam as a lone figure and the first natural man of God's creation. Now Adam was given a very specific assignment. He was told to be fruitful, multiply, replenish the earth and subdue it, and have dominion over the fish of the sea, the fowl of the air, and over every living thing that moved upon the earth (see Genesis 1:28). Small wonder God decided he couldn't do it alone!

If we view life as a game of sorts, it stands to reason that the greatest victories are won by teamwork, not by one player. We've all seen the demise of a team when one person decides to be the star and hog all the action. It makes the entire unit vulnerable to defeat. As King Solomon said, "Two are better than one, because they have a good return for their work" (Ecclesiastes 4:9). The benefits of having a partner to help you reach your goal are a positive reality.

Adam had been enjoying sweet fellowship with the Lord every evening in what had to be perfect utopia—the Garden of Eden. Yet God was the One to say that something was missing. He declared that it was not good for the man to be alone. Now let's consider the dynamics of His statement. Adam was not alone. He had God for company, as well as the rest of God's creation—animals, fish, and fowl. The earth teamed with life, and yet God concluded that Adam was alone. He was not a complete reflection of the Trinity because he was one in himself, not yet one with anyone else. Sharing his oneness was necessary for him to understand the mystery of oneness: the power of intimacy and what could be conceived by that union. He needed another to complete the picture of who he was.

WHEN GOD IS NOT ENOUGH

But isn't God supposed to be enough in our lives? Shouldn't we be satisfied with just Him? I can truly say that I am happy and fulfilled as a single and I revel in my relationship with God. My satisfaction comes from the relationship that He and I have built, *not* from a bitterness or some sense of resignation because nothing else has worked out for me. God has made His own special space in my heart and filled it to over-flowing. Some, however, in their disillu-sionment over past hurts and unfulfilling relationships, are quick to claim, "I don't need anyone else in my life anyway. I've got God." This is true, but the real truth lies in the attitude behind the claim. Though God does want to be our *first* love, the operative word being *first,* He *does not want us to select Him as our All in All because we can't find anything better.* This attitude speaks of a spirit that has grown callous from disappointment, not a heart that is joyfully sold out to the Lord of lords.

> *Men need help and so do women. This truth lays the foundation for being able to celebrate our differences and embrace them as positives that will assist us to live a fuller life.*

A heart that truly loves God and is whole because of rich interaction with Him thrives on loving others and lavishing upon others the love God has poured into our hearts. There is a delicate balance between delighting and resting in your relationship with God and shutting down your heart because your expectations of another person have been dashed. It is up to you to be honest with yourself. What is your motivation for seeking or shunning an intimate relationship?

God considered the mandate He had given Adam and made a decision concerning what Adam would need to effectively perform his tasks. Yes, it is true: Men need help and so do women. With this resolved, we find that one is not superior to the other. This truth lays the foundation for being able to celebrate our differences and embrace them as positives that will assist us to live a fuller life.

In the beginning God used wisdom, who is personified as a woman in the book of Proverbs, in establishing the creation (see 3:19). Wisdom says she was there at the very beginning and delighted in all that God created in His sovereignty. Wisdom was not *above* God and cannot work *apart* from Him, but as one of His attributes, she had great influence in what God was doing. Similarly, we are His helpers today, working to glorify Him and enlarge His kingdom on earth. God acknowledges our need for help. So who are we to say we don't need it? Everyone needs help.

Some might cite Paul and say that he didn't have a wife. Not only did he not have a wife, Paul was of the opinion that an unmarried man can do a better job of serving God than a married man (see 1 Corinthians 7:1,7,32-35). Though Paul is obviously not opposed to marriage, it seems from this particular passage that Paul thinks a man should marry only if he needs help controlling his sexual urges! I firmly believe that God knows which situation—the married or single life—suits a person best. Some are called to be single, as Paul, to remain focused on a very specific purpose for the Lord. These men and women will be given a peace to accompany that very special call. However, an unmarried man is not excluded from the calling of being a Proverbs 31 man. Plenty women will be affected by his presence, whether he is their friend or brother, coworker, or passing acquaintance. Single men, make note of the value that godly women will add to your life and embrace it. Even Paul was surrounded by sisters in the Lord who assisted him, encouraged him, and I'm sure prayed for him and comforted him with their continual support and valuable input in difficult moments.

God Himself works in partnership with Jesus and the Holy Spirit. Though the Three are One, each is a unique person, reflecting the fullness of God's character, with distinctly different characteristics and job assignments. The same is true of men and women. We also, when coupled with the Spirit of God as the missing link, mirror the Three in One, or Trinity of heaven.

Proof, you say? Fair enough. After making this corporate decision from heaven, God caused a deep sleep to come upon Adam and took from him a rib to fashion the woman. Upon completion, God presented Eve to Adam. We all know it was love at first sight as Adam exclaimed, "This is now bone of my bones and flesh of my flesh; she shall be called 'woman,' for she was taken out of man" (Genesis 2:23). Woman came *out* of man; therefore, she was a *part* of man. Part of the same body. The natural body does not refuse to work together. It understands that all parts must function to promote the whole.

> As it is, there are many parts, but one body.
>
> The eye cannot say to the hand, "I don't need you!" And the head cannot say to the feet, "I don't need you!" On the contrary, those parts of the body that seem to be weaker are indispensable, and the parts that we think are less honorable we treat with special honor. And the parts that are unpresentable are treated with special modesty, while our presentable parts need no special treatment. But God has combined the members of the body and has given greater honor to the parts that lacked it, so that there should be no division in the body, but that its parts should have equal concern for each other. If one part suffers, every part suffers with it; if one part is honored, every part rejoices with it.
>
> Now you are the body of Christ, and each one of you is a part of it. (1 Corinthians 12:20-27)

Adam recognized that Eve was a part of his very being, his own body. This was clear because he had done his homework. He had named all of the animals and learned how to exercise the authority God had given to him. He had discovered the power of his own words to establish things on earth. But while doing this he noticed that none of God's creatures were a match made in heaven for him. They just didn't complete him. They didn't look like him or have the same interests. They were a different species. But Eve! She was a different story.

True, some of her body parts were different, but he couldn't deny something familiar about her. Though different, she was very much like him at the same time. He felt the bond. He sensed the connection. Who knows—perhaps he even was conscious of the space that now existed in his rib cage and felt complete when he gazed at her. No one knows what impressions caused Adam to be so assured in his conclusion. Regardless, he knew Eve was for him and he was for her. In his mind, nothing would separate them from this moment forward. But he hadn't banked on one powerful force—sin. Though they were not physically separated after the Fall, we all feel the effects of the emotional chasm that came between man and woman that day when their blissful harmony was shattered by the sound of one solitary bite, or was it two?

The Ultimate Team

But in the beginning the plan was a good one; together they would be able to carry out God's assignment to man to be fruitful. Adam would plant the seed; Eve would give it birth. Together they would multiply their fruit, nurture it, and replenish the earth with new life. Together they would establish order or subdue all that transpired in the earth and have dominion by exercising their God-given authority over every living thing. This was truly about team effort.

The problem occurred when one member of the team, Eve, decided to become an independent agent. By choosing to reach for her own knowledge versus God's wisdom, she severed the intimate ties between her and God without realizing that her ties to Adam would also come unraveled. Sure enough, after being disobedient and partaking of the fruit that God had asked her not to eat, the verdict was delivered: "Your desire will be for your husband, and he will rule over you" (Genesis 3:16). Now that might appear to have upset the balance of the team if you don't get the full gist of what God was saying. Though Adam had been dubbed team captain, God was not saying that the woman would now be an inferior player. No. What He was saying was that now the woman would look to the man to fill the positions in her life that God had once filled. Since the man was not equipped to fill God's position, the woman's desire for the man to do so would rule over her. This was the birth of woman's unrealistic expectations toward man.

Man did not escape God's judgment either. God said to him, "Because you listened to your wife and ate from the tree about which I commanded you, 'You must not eat of it,' cursed is the ground because of you; through painful toil you will eat of it all the days of your life. It will produce thorns and thistles for you, and you will eat the plants of the field. By the sweat of your brow you will eat your food until you return to the ground, since from it you were taken; for dust you are and to dust you will return" (Genesis 3:17-19). In other

> *God's perfect design was for man to be the glory of God and the woman to be the glory of the man.*

words, because you, too, chose to be an independent agent, you will find it difficult to function in your position apart from Me.

Adam was also chastised because he had yielded to Eve's influence rather than protect her from her bad decision. Those of us who have younger siblings may remember who bore the consequences of misdeeds when we and the younger ones were disobedient. That's right, the older child. Why? Because we knew better and should have asserted our knowledge of the rules over the younger ones' impulses. Adam was responsible for leading and protecting Eve. In this regard he failed. His decision cost him the harmony he once knew with his wife, birthing distrust toward the woman. There you have it, ladies. Now you know why men won't heed your suggestion to ask for directions!

THE GAME OF LIFE

Was it God's design for men and women to be at odds? to make unrealistic demands of each other? to walk in distrust and a spirit of competition? Absolutely not! God's perfect design was for man to be the glory of God and the woman to be the glory of the man. What does that mean? Man was to represent the presence and power of God on earth. The woman was to reflect what the man reflected. If the man was in perfect fellowship with God, his life and all that he accomplished would be the manifestation of God's blessings. The woman by his side would reap these benefits and be a testimony of the man's obedience to God. What a team! They would both get to take the trophy home to enjoy and allow others to admire.

Let's consider the game of life in basketball terms. The man is the guard. He is responsible for bringing the ball down the court and setting up the play—in other words, coming up with the game plan. The guard looks for the best point of attack, judging which pass to which player yields the best chance for a score. He controls the ball until he can determine who is in the strongest position to shoot the ball. A truly confident man knows when to pass off a decision or a move to his wife if she is in a better position to score a point for the home team.

The woman plays the position of the forward. Though some forwards are called "small," they are no less formidable than any other player. On defense, forwards keep a constant eye on their opponents. This translates into a woman's making sure her man is covered and has all the room he needs to carry out the agreed-upon plan. On offense, forwards help the guard handle the ball. The woman helps the man move toward a winning play by balancing life between them. Forwards are also the players responsible for rebounding. Isn't that what women do? They can catch what might escape the man's grasp and turn things around, recovering and cre-

Though unisex is a cute theory, it is not one that works. Men and women are different, and those differences become their strengths when balancing the ball of life between them.

atively avoiding losses, keeping the home team winning. Women exercise discerning and intuitive muscle that keeps the team on point, foreseeing the advances of the opposition.

Obviously, God would be the center. This is where He belongs, in the middle of the court. Everything revolves around the center. The center occupies space in the middle of the defense. He is the great protector who makes it hard for the other team to score a point. That would be the enemy of your souls, Satan, who is highly opposed to man and woman being one. God also has the capacity to rebound.

Truly, God can seize our mistakes and losses and turn them for the good. It was God who rebounded the Fall of Adam and Eve in the garden. He made a sacrifice and covered them. It is God who can cover any mistakes you've made in your past or present relationship. Forwards and guards both are able to release to God what they cannot humanly accomplish. As you acknowledge the rules and your role in the game of love and life, He can recover your losses and set you back on the winning track.

FASHIONED BY DESIGN

That is the team that inspired God from the conception of time. It is still His perfect plan for man and woman to love together, work together, pray together, and win together. Satan, the opposition, will always try to dominate the court and pervert God's original game plan. He will magnify the human failings of both team members and cause them to be insecure. Insecurity makes us feel that we have to cover all the bases ourselves, and the boundaries of our God-designed roles become cloudy.

Though unisex is a cute theory, it is not one that works. Men and women are different, and those differences become their strengths when balancing the ball of life between them. One's weakness is the other's strength. Like pieces of a puzzle, these aspects fit together until everyone is finally able to see the big picture of how life should work between a man and a woman.

Couples cannot function in their respective roles effectively if one partner is always stepping on the other's toes. In God's great design the body never gets its parts confused. The finger doesn't try to act like the toe. Otherwise we'd all be tripping over ourselves. Winning teams are like fine-tuned bodies that have learned to appreciate each part's function and assignment without question. It is time to rejoice in our God-given roles and allow each other to play within the confines of our working positions. Then and only then will the game be won.

So man and woman are part of the same body, operating as a reflection of the triune Godhead in unity. What does this have to do with the aforementioned Proverbs 31 man? It has everything to do with him, because the Proverbs 31 man must know and understand who he is as a man. Who was he designed to be in God's mind? What does a woman need from him? The answers to these questions are multifaceted and will form the heart of the chapters to come. It is my heart's hope that you will gain not just information but true understanding. Understanding is part of the passage from boyhood to manhood and enables a man to take possession of his calling. Knowing your identity clarifies your assignment and clears the path toward your destiny.

I was going somewhere with two male friends of mine when one said something that really surprised me. The older said to the younger, "I decided to stop fooling around and get married when I realized that every successful man I knew was married. I had some single friends who were successful monetarily, but they just didn't seem to be as grounded or stable or even consistent in their success, monetarily or emotionally." I listened in stunned silence as he went on to encourage my younger friend to seriously consider settling down if he wanted his life to move forward. This man then went on to give his wife credit for his success. "I could never have done it without her," he said. "It was her presence in my life and the sobering realization of what I needed to do for my family that finally got me focused and on the right track."

The Proverbs 31 man loves women because he recognizes that they are a part of his very being. He does not have caustic thoughts or distrustful feelings toward women. He is secure in his maleness and does not wave it like a banner, but walks in it. He is not intimidated by a woman's strength because he is aware of his own strength, which is inherent in God's design. When secure in his purpose and his design, he can release his woman to be all that she can be. Together, as they stand side by side validated by God in their unique roles, they complement each other, overcome, and win the game.

Though one may be overpowered, two can defend themselves.
A cord of three strands is not quickly broken.

ECCLESIASTES 4:12

The Proverbs 31 man considers the woman in his life
to be an equal but unique partner.

FOR REFLECTION AND DISCUSSION

For Him

"He who finds a wife finds what is good and receives favor from the LORD" (Proverbs 18:22). A wife who is a helper in a man's life is a good thing. God uses the woman in your life to take you to the next level of success on every front—emotionally, spiritually, and financially.

- How comfortable are you in your masculinity? On what occasions do you question yourself? In what ways might your relationship with your father have shaped these ideas?

- Have you allowed God to affirm your manhood and define who you are in His eyes?

- How much of your life are you willing to share with a woman?

- Can you allow her to flourish in her own right without feeling threatened? What do you need from her in order to do this?

- Define your purpose in your wife's life. Are you fulfilling your role as a team player in her life?

For Her

"A wife of noble character who can find? She is worth far more than rubies. Her husband has full confidence in her and lacks nothing of value. She brings him good, not harm, all the days of her life" (Proverbs 31:10-12). One measurement of whether a woman is "a good thing" is what she can contribute to her husband's life. A woman who adds wisdom and blessing to a man's life is priceless.

- Consider what you have to offer to a godly man. How much do you give? How much do you withhold? Why? What stops the flow of the goodness that you could pour out?

- Do you have a problem with authority or the word *submission?* Why?
- Do you see the man in your life as a teammate or a dictator? Is this view real or imagined?
- How can you help the man in your life? How can you hurt or hinder the man in your life?
- Are you secure in your femininity? Do you rejoice in your weaknesses as well as your strengths?
- How has your relationship with your father affected your view of yourself as a woman? Have you allowed God to affirm you as a woman?

For You Both

A man and a woman who understand their unique strengths and how they contribute to each other make a powerful team that impacts not only their home but their community.

- Make a list of what you would like to accomplish in life. What type of help will you need? How can you constructively help each other achieve your goals?
- Are you able to view each other as wonderful complements? How do you see this dynamic played out in your relationship?
- Are you willing to allow each other to exercise your individual strengths? How do you see these adding to your relationship?
- How much are you willing to yield to each other in the decision-making process?
- Do you trust each other to make choices for the betterment of you both at all times? Why? And how does that trust get disrupted? What could solidify it?

4

LEAVING AND CLEAVING

Establishing Your Priorities

...go to my country and my own relatives
and get a wife for my son Isaac.

GENESIS 24:4

> The Proverbs 31 man is able to prioritize the issues
> in his life and deal with them accordingly.

There is definitely a time when a man's got to do what a man's got to do. The Proverbs 31 man knows the stakes of life are high. He knows the decisions he makes will affect his destiny.

Whether you make the decision to live a saved and sanctified life exclusively unto the Lord or venture into the mystery of becoming one with another in marriage, the decisions you make today will definitely affect your tomorrow. Whether single or married, your decisions should never be made from the throne of your own selfish desires, but from heavenly priorities. This demands focus on the call of God.

Being of a happy, sanguine temperament, I have to confess that I am easily given to distraction. But I have learned over the years that too much flexibility is not conducive to reaching my goals or keeping what I have gained. Decisions must be made and adhered to. Boundaries must be put in place. Most of all, priorities must be held high. The Proverbs 31 man plans his work and works his plan in business and in life. He makes adjustments to accommodate change. He knows the perfect order of his life: His relationship with God first, his family second, work and career third. For the single man it is God first, the relationships where God has called him to serve second, and career third. Both are called to be godly leaders within their sphere of influence. Therefore, the following principles still apply to those who do not have a family at this time. As you practice them in your singleness, you will be more prepared for married life.

God will never give a woman a calling that is in competition or conflict with her husband's life assignment. God is not the author of confusion; the human ego is.

You might ask, *Where do you get this order regarding priorities? Do you have Scripture for that?* Let's look at Paul's mandate for a man who was to be an overseer of the church. It is safe to say that those same requirements apply to every godly man, no matter what his profession. "An overseer, then, must be above reproach, the husband of one wife, temperate, prudent, respectable, hospitable, able to teach, not addicted to wine or pugnacious, but gentle, peaceable, free from the love of money. He must be one who manages his own household well, keeping his children under control with all dignity (but if a man does not know how to manage his own household, how will he take care of the church of God?)" (1 Timothy 3:2-5, NASB). The principle at work here: If you can't keep your house or your relationships in order, how will you keep your business in order? Feelings of security that come from attention, nurturing, and discipline work together with love to establish order in a home. It is safe to say that the atmosphere changes in a house when daddy is home and is an active player in what transpires within.

I am speaking, of course, of the order of the heart. God does not desire to replace the attention that a man must pay to his loved ones. In other words, when a man lives first to please God, he treats his woman and his family as he should. Because he treats his family properly, he is crowned with favor that causes him to succeed in his career. This is the order of God. In this way family does not become a god, but neither does a man's work. Each has its rightful place in his heart. For the single, nurturing healthy relationships keeps life in perspective and priorities in the right order. Therefore, transitions to married life will be less difficult.

A HUSBAND'S SACRIFICE

After Sarah died, Abraham decided it was time for Isaac, his son, to take a wife. She had to come from among his people, which can be translated in a modern context to mean she had to be a believer. Abraham's servant asked whether Isaac should go to her if she was unwilling to leave her family; the answer was a resounding no. She must be willing to leave her country and family to forge a new life with Isaac. Why? Because Isaac had a divine calling on his life, and location was important.

Abraham told his servant, "The LORD, the God of heaven, who brought me out of my father's household and my native land and who spoke to me and promised me on oath, saying, 'To your offspring I will give this land'—he will send his angel before you so that you can get a wife for my son from there" (Genesis 24:7).

Now I see some women asking, "So *I'm* the one who has to leave? Well, what about *my* calling?" You might not like my answer, but that doesn't make it any less true: Because of the order of God that I discussed in chapter 3, God will never give you a calling that is in competition or conflict with your husband's life assignment. God is not the author of confusion; the human ego is. If He has placed a high call on your life in business or in ministry, He will give you a man who will support and celebrate your gifts. If not, you must be willing to wait on God's timing and position to be released into the things you feel in your heart you have been called to do. God will use your husband as a barometer and timer in your life. Relax in that security and wait on the Lord to open the door for you.

Back to Isaac. It was crucial that his wife (1) be from his country, (2) be from his people, and (3) be willing to follow her husband. Abraham's servant, symbolic of the Holy Spirit in this story, also added the additional requirement that she must have a heart to serve (see Genesis 24:14).

The wife a Proverbs 31 man seeks is a woman who comes from his country, one who has a similar background and values. He looks for a woman from among his people, one who is a believer, and one who is willing to follow him. Such a wife will allow him to be the leader God expects him to be. Which brings me to my point.

A woman is asked to sacrifice a lot in becoming a wife, to the point of yielding her life to a man. Nothing less is expected of the man. He, too, must make a great sacrifice. The Proverbs 31 man knows and understands that when he takes a wife she becomes his number one priority after his relationship with and obedience to God. This mandate comes from God, who says, "Husbands, love your wives, just as Christ loved the church and gave himself up for her" (Ephesians 5:25). In other words, be willing to die for her sake. He takes it a step further by instructing, "In this same way, husbands ought to love their wives as their own bodies. He who loves his wife loves himself" (verse 28). In other words, do for her what you would do for yourself. And this admonition is sobering: "Husbands, in the same way be considerate as you live with your wives, and treat them with respect as the weaker partner and as heirs with you of the gracious gift of life, so that nothing will hinder your prayers" (1 Peter 3:7). Whoa! This is serious! How precious a woman must be in God's sight if He would hold up her husband's prayer requests until he treats his wife properly! Why don't we hear that one preached from pulpits more often?

What is God really saying? Men, treat your wives first with consideration; you are responsible for her well-being. We believers collectively are the bride of Christ. We are God's priority over everything else in His creation. He was willing to sacrifice His own Son to restore our intimate relationship with Him, thus sealing our state of well-being. He assures our position in righteousness, that is, "right standing" with Him. He asks the same of natural man when dealing with his natural bride.

ONE PLUS ONE EQUALS ONE

I find it interesting that Abraham chose to look for a wife for Isaac after Sarah's death. Could it be that Isaac was a mama's boy? That would make sense. Born to Sarah in her old age, he would have become everything to her.

Would strife have arisen in the camp if Isaac had taken a wife sooner? Probably. Sarah would have been busy instructing this woman in the right way to care for her son. Would Isaac have expected Rebekah to be like his mother and then discovered she was not, causing problems between them? Probably. It is a natural reaction to want more of what you have been used to. Would he have had to deal with his mother constantly pointing out the failures of his new wife? Probably. It's a mother thing, generally speaking. Poor Isaac would have been stuck in the middle, trying to keep the peace between mother and wife. That's not a good position, yet many modern men find themselves in this very dilemma. Even so, God is clear: "For this reason a man will leave his father and mother and be united to his wife, and they will become one flesh" (Genesis 2:24). This is a scripture that many mothers need to accept as well; many mothers find it hard to let go of their sons, especially when they make their sons into surrogate husbands because they are not emotionally fulfilled in their own marriages.

The text says in Genesis 24:67 that upon Rebekah's arrival Isaac married her, took her into his mother's tent, and loved her. Rebekah,

> *Why does God command men to love their wives while simply telling women to respect and submit to their husbands? In His foreknowledge, perhaps He knew these would be the greatest two issues in marriage.*

not Sarah, became Isaac's new focus and priority. The Proverbs 31 man understands his wife is neither his mother nor his "buddy." He is able to make the separation; accordingly, he is able to adjust his expectations as well as his understanding of his own responsibilities toward his wife.

One flesh means that the woman becomes a part of the man she marries. Her life is as valuable as his own. He is to guard it and protect it with his life. When Jacob took his family from his father-in-law's house and headed out on his own, he was told that his brother was coming toward him with a huge army. Believing Esau was coming to settle an old score, the first thing he did was move his two wives (sorry, guys, this is no longer allowed) and family out of harm's way. He made sure they were out of the line of fire and went to face Esau alone (see Genesis 33:1-3).

Boaz, upon deciding to make Ruth his wife, immediately sought to protect her reputation by having her leave the threshing floor before light so that no one would see her and start the rumor that she had visited him for a midnight tryst (see Ruth 3:14).

Joseph, upon learning that Mary, the mother of Jesus, was with child, sought to put her away quietly so that she would not be stoned for fornication (see Matthew 1:19). Each of these men had a deep sense of responsibility toward the woman in their lives. They were aware of their obligation to protect her heart, her body, her emotions, and her reputation. These men also knew how to separate themselves from their childhood families and forge new paths with the woman they had joined themselves with. They embraced the principle of leaving and cleaving.

The two becoming one means that parts of both partners must die so that as one they can truly live. There is no space for selfishness at the marriage altar. I find many times that I slip and make the mistake of calling weddings funerals, and yet it is true. Two people must die to individual agendas in order to inhabit one body comfortably. There is simply not room for two. Two sets of rights, ideas, and agendas must be melted down in the cauldron of God's Spirit in order for a couple to focus on a mutual vision that will enhance both of their lives.

Why does God command men to love their wives while simply telling women to respect and submit to their husbands? In His foreknowledge, perhaps He knew these would be the greatest two issues in marriage. What do women crave from men more than anything? Not money, not trinkets—love. What does a man want from his wife more than anything? Not sex, not food—honor and respect. Here's a secret to both people getting what they want: Men, the leader in you can choose to make the initial sacrifice of doing what it takes to make your wife feel loved. This must become a priority. If this does not come naturally, exert the effort. But the reward of your labor will be a woman who willingly submits because she feels cherished and protected.

> *Here's a secret to both people getting what they want: Men, the leader in you can choose to make the initial sacrifice.... The reward of your labor will be a woman who willingly submits.*

In my travels I speak with a lot of couples. The number one complaint among men is wives who are unresponsive to their intimate physical desires. I usually find that the wives in question have been harboring hurt and anger because they have not received the love and understanding they need from their husbands, or the women feel betrayed by their husbands in some way. The nature of a woman is to respond to love—to open like a flower blossom in response to treatment that makes her feel special. That makes her feel as if she is a priority in a man's life. This garners her trust and lets her know that her heart and her life are safe in his hands.

When the Proverbs 31 man crowns his wife queen, she in turn crowns him king. Remember that when Esther appeared before her king with an urgent request, he did not allow work to distract him from the needs of his wife. Everything stopped. After all, wouldn't it still be there when he returned? He stopped what he was doing and focused on his wife. In return, his own needs for sustenance and attention were met (see Esther 5:2-7).

WORK TO LIVE

Many men, because they find their sense of identity in their work, have a tendency to put their work before the woman in their life, not realizing that they lose ground on both fronts when they do this. Obviously, God felt strongly enough about this to write this law: "If a man has recently married, he must not be sent to war or have any other duty laid on him. For one year he is to be free to stay at home and bring happiness to the wife he has married" (Deuteronomy 24:5). That is serious. War is a most crucial time, yet God says, take a break and honeymoon for a year before getting back into the swing of things. Take care of business at home before trying to take care of business in the streets.

The work ethic set forth by God's principles is simple: The object of having an occupation is that we work to live, not live to work. Life does not consist of a man's or woman's work. Apart from God, a man has to strive harder to reap a return for his efforts. But that is life under the curse. In the blessed life, a man in partnership with God gains a good reward for his labor minus the stress, because God is on his side. This partnership with God frees him to love his woman as he should. He in turn is revitalized by her ministering response, which equips him to function even better in the marketplace. Why? Because every component of his life—his relationship with God, with his wife, with work—is being fulfilled, which makes him sound in mind and body.

The more common scenario, unfortunately, is a workaholic husband who feels nagged by his wife because she constantly complains about the time he doesn't spend with his family. She shuts down emotionally and is not interested in being intimate with him. This messes with his mind and robs him of the focus he needs to function effectively at work. The vicious cycle begins and more often than not is never corrected. The break comes when the man loses his job, his wife, or both. Or the wife loses her husband to a woman who seems more understanding at the time. Even so, if the man does not correct the pattern that led him to this place, he'll soon find himself in the same position with his second wife.

Prioritizing is crucial to the life of every man. God first, wife and family second. All else falls behind these two things that equip and empower him to be a man who will be spoken well of in the gates. Please don't be overwhelmed or confused. Remember, this order is about the attitude of the heart rather than a physical to-do list. As you ask God daily to give you wisdom, He will guide you in prioritizing the demands on your life. On some days your family will need less, and attention to the details of your career or ministry will require more, but God is the great balancer. Seek Him for direction. The key is to be both flexible and sensitive to the leading of the Holy Spirit. Everything has its place in our lives and a season when one thing or the other will demand more of your attention. The Proverbs 31 .man, however, knows how to consider all that is before him and proceed with everything in divine order.

———

*In this same way, husbands ought to love their wives
as their own bodies. He who loves his wife loves himself.
After all, no one ever hated his own body, but he feeds
and cares for it, just as Christ does the church.*

EPHESIANS 5:28-29

**The Proverbs 31 man places God and his wife
above all other things.**

FOR REFLECTION AND DISCUSSION

For Him

"Here is a trustworthy saying: If anyone sets his heart on being an overseer, he desires a noble task. Now the overseer must be above reproach, the husband of but one wife, temperate, self-controlled, respectable, hospitable, able to teach, not given to drunkenness, not violent but gentle, not quarrelsome, not a lover of money. He must manage his own family well and see that his children obey him with proper respect. (If anyone does not know how to manage his own family, how can he take care of God's church?)" (1 Timothy 3:1-5). Though this scripture refers to the qualifications for a bishop, every man is called to be the bishop or overseer of his home. He must walk in the realization that the submission of his wife and the obedience of his children are reliant on his capacity to make them feel secure in his love.

- If you are considering marriage, are you ready to die to all other distractions and put the woman in your life first?
- If married, do you make the security of your wife—heart, body, and soul—first on your list of priorities? What are you doing to make this evident in your home?
- Do you struggle with your identity in the workplace? Are you given to being a workaholic? If yes, why do you think this is?
- How do you believe God has called you to balance your desire for achievement with your obligations to home?
- Make a list of romantic surprises you can pull off to make your wife feel loved.

For Her

"In the same way, their wives are to be women worthy of respect, not malicious talkers but temperate and trustworthy in everything" (1 Timothy 3:11). "Wives, in the same way be submissive to your husbands so that, if any of them do not believe the word, they may be won over without words by the behavior of their wives" (1 Peter 3:1). Ladies, never expect what you do not earn; your husband's love must be cultivated. Become the type of woman your man wants to place above all other things in his life.

- If single, do you see evidence that you are a priority in the life of the man you are considering for a mate? How he begins is how he will end.
- If married, has the pattern of your husband changed in the area of attentiveness? In what way? Do you know the cause? Do you feel as if you are a top priority in his life?
- What things can you change in your manner to make him want to step into his rightful place?
- How have you changed in your interactions with your husband since you got married?
- Do you love the man in your life enough to do the work it takes to become his number one priority?

For You Both

When men and women set their priorities in godly order, they can become an effective force in every area of their lives.

- How willing are you to be distracted from your personal goals to deal with the needs of your partner? What void does your career or other activities fill that your mate doesn't?

How can you help each other to balance your needs and priorities?

- What can you do to make your mate feel more loved? What areas have you overlooked in the past?
- Are any of your spouse's complaints or insecurities valid? What can you do to correct these issues?
- What things does your spouse vocalize that you have ignored or not thought were critical?
- Make a plan and set aside a special time for cultivating your love relationship.

5

THE LIVING PROOF

Standing on Principle

Teach me your way, O LORD, and I will walk in your truth;
give me an undivided heart, that I may fear your name.

PSALM 86:11

A Proverbs 31 man is honest in his commitments
and devotes himself wholeheartedly to them.

Let us continue the discussion of a man's work—the work of home and the work of business. The man who lacks integrity at work cannot be trusted at home. Just as salt and fresh water cannot flow from the same fountain, honesty and integrity cannot flow from the same heart that harbors lies and deceit (see James 3:11). "The good man brings good things out of the good stored up in his heart, and the evil man brings evil things out of the evil stored up in his heart. For out of the overflow of his heart his mouth speaks" (Luke 6:45). The integrity, persistence, and consistency that a man displays at work are the same attitudes he will display at home.

A Proverbs 31 man follows through on his commitments and walks in honesty. He does not make excuses, shirk responsibility, or resort to dishonest behavior in times of stress. He perseveres in his relationships as well as his work.

NOW THAT'S DEDICATION!

As I mentioned earlier, Daniel was such an honest man that no one could find any dirty laundry to expose when they sought to undermine his godly reputation. He was steadfast in his integrity. But what about the more normal sort of guy? The kind most women meet every day, who has a history of sorts, who hasn't always played by the book—is it possible for him to become this type of man? Most definitely!

Jacob, whose name means "supplanter" or "deceiver," is a prime example of how choosing to live a life of integrity and consistency can reap tremendous favor from God and change your entire destiny. Here is a young man who came into the world with a sense of entitlement, grasping from the beginning for things that he decided he should have (see Genesis 25:26). He even schemed his way into robbing his older brother Esau of the birthright and blessing of the firstborn (see Genesis 25:29-34;27:1-40). He did whatever it took to get what he wanted, and he got away with it, too. For a time.

But one day Jacob met his match. First he had a life-changing encounter with God (see Genesis 28:10-22). Then he came face to face with a woman he loved, Rachel (see Genesis 29:9-12). Neither the blessings of God nor Rachel was going to be easy for him to obtain. No manipulation would work in this situation. Jacob the liar was about to be broken so that he could become the prince, Israel, that he was born to be.

Upon spotting Rachel, Jacob made a decision. This was the woman whom he would marry. I've heard modern renditions of this story often enough to be convinced that generally speaking a man knows his intentions toward a woman early on, sometimes at first sight. Jacob went to her father and asked for her hand, pledging to work for his father-in-law for seven years as a bride price.

Not only does the Proverbs 31 man know and recognize his bride, he understands that there is a price to be paid for the hand of a woman and the privilege of enjoying intimacy with her. In our instant-gratification society, it is hard to imagine two people who loved each other so intensely that they would wait so long for the privilege to come together, but they did. However, something terrible happened first. Jacob became a victim of the same devices he had used early in his life. Laban, Rachel's father, pulled a switch on the wedding night and gave Leah, Rachel's older sister, to Jacob instead.

> *The love of a woman, coupled with a reverence for God, made Jacob an honest man. Jacob's wife did not change him; his love for her did.*

Did Jacob lose it? The Bible doesn't give us the inside scoop on his reaction. The more incredible point, however, is that Jacob vowed to work *another* seven years in order to marry Rachel as well! Not even this disastrous setback could make him break the commitment he had made to the woman he loved. Nor did he allow adverse conditions to bow his spirit.

Jacob served seven years to get Rachel, but they seemed like only a few days to him because of his love for her.

Then Jacob said to Laban, "Give me my wife. My time is completed, and I want to lie with her."

So Laban brought together all the people of the place and gave a feast. But when evening came, he took his daughter Leah and gave her to Jacob, and Jacob lay with her. And Laban gave his servant girl Zilpah to his daughter as her maidservant.

When morning came, there was Leah! So Jacob said to Laban, "What is this you have done to me? I served you for Rachel, didn't I? Why have you deceived me?"

Laban replied, "It is not our custom here to give the younger daughter in marriage before the older one. Finish this daughter's bridal week; then we will give you the younger one also, in return for another seven years of work."

And Jacob did so. He finished the week with Leah, and then Laban gave him his daughter Rachel to be his wife. (Genesis 29:20-28)

Fourteen years he worked for Rachel's hand in marriage. Now that's what I call commitment! Many men might not give up at the first sign of difficulty in their relationship with a woman, but few have Jacob's tenacity. How many take a woman's stand on holiness, for example, as personal rejection rather than an indication of a godly woman he will be able to respect and trust in marriage? For those single women who have grown discouraged in this area, let me say that the man who is worthy of your love is the man who is willing to work to gain your trust and to wait to share the marriage bed with you. He should take the position of being responsible for protecting you from falling.

CHANGED BY THE LOVE, NOT BY THE WOMAN

After the passion of the courtship and wedding, how does the Proverbs 31 man view his responsibility toward the woman he has claimed as his own? After Jacob married Rachel and Leah, he continued to work for Laban for years—through the births of twelve children! Jacob, through his trials, had grown into a responsible man. He shouldered the weight of caring for his new family. He was now called to be a provider, and provide he would. We must give Jacob additional credit for maintaining his marital commitment to Leah when he might have cast her off because he did not love her. (He certainly must have desired peace from the constant competition and fighting between his two sister wives!) Yet he did not do this even after he left Laban. Well aware that he could not just take his family and go back home to nothing, he bided his time, putting his pride aside, until the opportune moment. He then went to his father-in-law and said,

> "Give me my wives and children, for whom I have served you, and I will be on my way. You know how much work I've done for you."
>
> But Laban said to him, "If I have found favor in your eyes, please stay. I have learned by divination that the LORD has blessed me because of you." He added, "Name your wages, and I will pay them."

Jacob said to him, "You know how I have worked for you and how your livestock has fared under my care. The little you had before I came has increased greatly, and the LORD has blessed you wherever I have been. But now, when may I do something for my own household?"

"What shall I give you?" he asked.

"Don't give me anything," Jacob replied. "But if you will do this one thing for me, I will go on tending your flocks and watching over them: Let me go through all your flocks today and remove from them every speckled or spotted sheep, every dark-colored lamb and every spotted or speckled goat. They will be my wages. And my honesty will testify for me in the future, whenever you check on the wages you have paid me." (Genesis 30:26-33)

"And my honesty will testify for me..." Whoa! What a turnaround! It is safe to say that the love of a woman, coupled with a reverence for God, had made Jacob an honest man. His question to Laban is also revealing: "But now, when may I do something for my own household?" In other words, it's been great working for you, Dad, but I need to focus on my family now." The spoiled brat had become a responsible man.

I must make a note here that Jacob's wife did not change him; his love for her did. There is a big difference. Many women believe they can change a man, and when they begin to attempt to rearrange his mind and spirit, they are met with resistance. This is never a good approach. Ladies, decide what you can and cannot live with before committing to marriage. No man is perfect, so determine your non-negotiables ahead of time and make your decision accordingly. Sometimes the problem is not in the man; it's in us. Be open to God's counsel and remain flexible. As He accomplishes a transforming work in your own heart, you might become pleasantly surprised by the changes birthed in that man as a response to the change in you. If you are the woman who fills his heart as you should, he will want to be his very best for you and adjust himself accordingly. Because of Jacob's great love for Rachel, he became a work in progress out of his desire to please her, not because of what she demanded.

Even so, God was not yet finished breaking him in order to make him a mighty leader of Israel.

WHERE CHANGE MEETS ACTION

If there was any dishonesty left in Jacob, God used Laban to root it out. Laban gave Jacob a taste of his own medicine so that he would never again consider being deceitful to gain his own way. Laban, spurred by his jealousy of how God prospered Jacob, changed his son-in-law's wages ten times and developed an attitude. Still Jacob persevered until the Lord told him it was time to leave (see Genesis 31:1-10).

Following the word of the Lord, Jacob prepared to take his family back to his homeland. His wives readily agreed with him, citing all the times their father had deceived Jacob and dealt unfairly with him. Jacob packed up his family and headed for the hills, so to speak. This was his last streak of deceit, as he did not tell Laban he was leaving. Laban came after him, but he was stopped from doing Jacob any harm by a strong warning from the Lord in a dream. After Laban accused him of dishonesty, Jacob was quick to point out all that he had endured from Laban for twenty years (see Genesis 31:22-31,38-44). What an incredible picture: two schemers, face to face, demanding honesty from each other. It had to be ironic to Jacob.

The last rite of passage that Jacob would endure was a wrestling match with the angel of the Lord (Genesis 32:22-31). Jacob would be forever changed by this experience, in name as well as in character and body. (God dislocated Jacob's hip as they wrestled, leaving him with a permanent limp as a reminder of their encounter.) He would from that day forward be known as Israel, meaning, "One who strives with God and perseveres." It was a humbler Jacob who fathered and established the famous tribes of Israel. This truth is further demonstrated in Jacob's reunion with Esau; though Isaac had said Jacob would rule over Esau, Jacob repeatedly refers to Esau as "my lord" and himself as "your servant." How amazing is that?!

Every man comes to a point in his own life when he wrestles with the demons within. The Proverbs 31 man submits himself to the hand of God, allowing Him to purge him of all that is not conducive to godly manhood. At this point, such a man can stand tall and walk with a new sobriety, even if with a limp, through life. He emerges aware of his calling from God as well as his responsibility to be the priest and leader of his home. For some, the wrestling match must occur before he can know his purpose in life, simply because he must come to the end of himself in order to be open to God's plan. But for most, the wrestling match comes after the revelation, when the last vestiges of fears and even personal agendas are surrendered to the only One who can truly be Lord, God Himself. Only after arriving at this strong but vulnerable place can a man allow

> *One of the most important components of one's integrity is the ability to follow through with a commitment no matter what the cost.*

God, as well as his wife, to keep him honest in conviction, attitude, and action. He knows that the people he commits himself to will in turn commit to him.

HONESTY BEFORE MARRIAGE

Not every man is willing to give his all for a woman. Some, when they become aware of what it costs, decline and move on. As long as they can enjoy the benefits of a relationship without the responsibility of marriage, they will partake of whatever a woman will give. As I mentioned in chapter 3, many men today delay committing to marriage until much later in life. One university survey concluded that men wait to marry because they can enjoy all the benefits of married life—namely sex—outside of marriage, so why bother? But when a woman lets a man know there is a price to be paid for her love—as in the commitment of marriage—the party's over! Again, if you are a woman who has experienced this, do not take his choice personally. Rather, know it is the man who has lost something priceless. At the same time, don't push a man into marriage if he's not ready. You could carry the relationship for the rest of your life if you do. And, men, as I always say, if you're not ready for prime-time television, don't turn it on.

A man's willingness to communicate his intentions or feelings to a woman is crucial to the success or progress of their relationship. When Jacob met Rachel, he made his intentions clear. She did not have to do any guesswork about his feelings. She arrived to water her sheep, he rolled the well stone away, he kissed her, and the rest was history! He went to her father and asked if he could work to earn her hand in marriage.

The woman in a man's life should never be left to speculate on where she fits in that man's life. She should never have to wonder what his intentions are toward her. If you mutually agree to the terms of the relationship, then you must stand on the premise you've stated. If it changes, be up front about it.

The imagination is a dangerous thing. It is almost never accurate when trying to gauge another person's feelings or objectives. So roll away the stone, men. Move distractions and hindrances in your relationship with your woman out of the way. Offer the refreshing waters of transparency and honesty to the one you care about. If you are not considering her to be a part of your future, she needs to know! God does not take kindly to a man's playing with a woman's affections and leading her on or vice versa.

Paying the Cost

One of the most important components of one's integrity is the ability to follow through with a commitment no matter what the cost. Boaz was well aware of the price he would have to pay in order to make Ruth his wife, and he was willing to pay it (see Ruth 3:9-13). But before he could marry Ruth, he had to talk to the rightful successor for her hand. Someone before him in the family lineup had the first right to redeem her and make her his wife. Boaz went to him and said,

> "Naomi, who has come back from Moab, is selling the piece of land that belonged to our brother Elimelech. I thought I should bring the matter to your attention and suggest that you buy it in the presence of these seated here and in the presence of the elders

of my people. If you will redeem it, do so. But if you will not, tell me, so I will know. For no one has the right to do it except you, and I am next in line."

"I will redeem it," he said.

Then Boaz said, "On the day you buy the land from Naomi and from Ruth the Moabitess, you acquire the dead man's widow, in order to maintain the name of the dead with his property."

At this, the kinsman-redeemer said, "Then I cannot redeem it because I might endanger my own estate. You redeem it yourself. I cannot do it." (Ruth 4:3-6)

You see, as long as this man was focused on what he would get out of the deal, he was ready to pay up, but the moment he was made aware of the full implications of what he was taking, his tune changed. He already had a wife and did not want the possibility of disharmony in his home. He went from considering the value of the land to the cost of marrying Ruth, which is what every man should do. If a man is not willing to pay the cost, or if he determines that he might not be adding value to that woman's life, he should make an honest assessment of whether he is up to the commitment or not.

> *Many make the decision to marry without counting the cost, even though the Bible plainly encourages us to do so before making life-altering decisions.*

I had a beau tell me once that I deserved a man better than himself. At the time I disagreed, but in hindsight I appreciated the fact that he cared enough about me to sacrifice a relationship that was more beneficial to him than it was to me. He knew that I would not be happy in the relationship long before I was able to discern this for myself. Eventually, my unhappiness would have made him unhappy as well. He was smart and honest enough to do the right thing and release me to eventually embrace a man who could love me the way he knew I deserved to be loved.

Many make the decision to marry without counting the cost, even though the Bible plainly encourages us to do so before making life-altering decisions. The price of a wedding can vary depending on how elaborate the ceremony. But the cost of a marriage is an entirely different subject. The real cost involves persevering through the good and the bad, for richer or for poorer, in sickness and in health, through weight gain and job loss, through difficult children, and during seasons of dryness and lack of passion. Ah, but if you don't grow weary of doing good, at the right time you will reap abundance (see Galatians 6:9).

Boaz got his woman, and their relationship was a fruitful one. They became the great-grandparents of David the king and are in the lineage of Jesus Christ. Boaz deserves extra credit here, because he had the insight to see past the prejudice that was prevalent in Israel toward Ruth's people. He could have disqualified her as the suitable partner based on her background. She was a Moabite. Moabites were the detested enemies of Israel. She, in the eyes of many, was nothing more than a godless foreigner. But Ruth had chosen the God of Israel to be her God. Her virtue shone through in the way she committed herself to her mother-in-law, Naomi (see Ruth 2:11-12).

Ruth's strong work ethic also spoke for her. Ladies, take a clue: You never know who's watching. Ruth was willing to do whatever was necessary in order to go on with the business of living and to provide for herself and her widowed mother-in-law. Her flawless reputation preceded her. But so did Boaz's experience in life. His mother had been a foreigner, not so highly regarded. His mother had been Rahab, a harlot, who had hidden the spies when they came to check out Jericho (see Joshua 2). His heart was already predisposed to have compassion for her and see past her race. He knew firsthand what it meant to be an outsider. This

> *A man who allows God to mold his heart will be a man prepared to receive God's best for him, though it might come in an unexpected package.*

should encourage any woman who feels as if her past or ethnic persuasion dictates her future when it comes to finding a mate. God has a man whom He has prepared just for you, a man who understands the road you have traveled. He will have a special sensitivity to your needs. He will protect you and love away all of your past pain, fear, and disappointments. He will be a Proverbs 31 man.

A man who allows God to mold his heart will be a man prepared to receive God's best for him, though it might come in an unexpected package. A man of integrity stays true to God's purposes rather than being ruled by circumstances or personal expectations. Consider Joseph, who was betrothed to Mary the mother of Jesus. How easy would it have been for him to call the whole engagement off after finding out that Mary was pregnant and bearing the Son of God, no less! It takes a special man to say, "All right, I can deal with that." Joseph planned to put her away privately and spare her the shame of a public divorce and the threat of stoning, as required by the Law of Moses. But the Lord intervened on Mary's behalf, and Joseph obeyed the Lord's instruction to marry her. Thank God for a man who can hear from on high and obey!

The average man has proud visions of being the father of his own children. He chafes at the thought of having to provide for those who are not his own. Sometimes an incredible woman is left standing alone with her children because a man does not want to bear the cost. Yet a Proverbs 31 man has a heart that has been enlarged by God to embrace those who are, in principle, not his responsibility. He assumes the posture that if those children are part of this woman he loves, then he will take the whole and gladly pay the cost.

I think of my own father, Mr. McKinney, who adopted me when he married my mother. The thought never occurred to anyone that I was not his natural child. To this day, he has been generous to me materially as well as emotionally. The cost of raising me was never a deterrent to the commitment he made to my mother. When I was miraculously reunited with my biological father, Mr. Hammond, my adopted father didn't pass me off like a football. He stayed in the game. Together they made decisions regarding my life and discipline without any strife.

When my natural father found me, he immediately chose to shoulder his responsibility for all that my life entailed. He never had the attitude that I had been doing great up to that point, so his help wasn't needed. No! He thanked my mother and the man who had lovingly fathered me thus far for all they had done, asked what he could do to help, and plunged in. I feel blessed to have not one but two Proverbs 31 men in my life as shining examples of what I should be looking for in a man.

In Africa there is a tribe that considers the ways of a man when he dies. If he did not take care of his wife and his children, they bury him face down as a sign of disgrace. Many men today have left women standing to bear the weight of raising children alone. This is not the heart of God. This is not the heart of the Proverbs 31 man. His mandate is clear, and he will stick to his assignment no matter what. He does not run from responsibility; he embraces it. His work ethic is one of performing with integrity, whether at home or in the world, and for this his wife and children rise and call him blessed.

———

Even in darkness light dawns for the upright, for the gracious and compassionate and righteous man. Good will come to him who is generous and lends freely, who conducts his affairs with justice. Surely he will never be shaken; a righteous man will be remembered forever. He will have no fear of bad news; his heart is steadfast, trusting in the LORD.

PSALM 112:4-7

The Proverbs 31 man garners
the trust of his wife and family
and the respect of his community,
because he follows through
with his commitments.

FOR REFLECTION AND DISCUSSION

For Him

"LORD, who may dwell in your sanctuary? Who may live on your holy hill? He whose walk is blameless and who does what is righteous, who speaks the truth from his heart" (Psalm 15:1-2). "Love and faithfulness meet together; righteousness and peace kiss each other" (Psalm 85:10). Truly when a man chooses to do the right thing, he finds the love and peace that his heart seeks.

- How faithful are you to your commitments? What deters you from keeping them? What can you do to correct this?
- What disciplines would be required of you at work that would make you achieve a higher level of success? at home?
- How honest are you? What causes you to lie or bend the truth?
- In what areas do you need to apply the art of perseverance? What stops you from doing it now?
- How can you best honor God concerning your family? as a single man?

For Her

"Truthful lips endure forever, but a lying tongue lasts only a moment" (Proverbs 12:19). "Many a man claims to have unfailing love, but a faithful man who can find?" (Proverbs 20:6). Many women, desperate to have a man, do not consider a man's true character and reap only temporary happiness. But the woman who insists on integrity will find lasting peace with her marriage partner.

- If single, how much time do you take to consider a man's character before you give your heart away? Has this led to disappointment? What can you do differently?

- If married, do you exhibit the integrity you desire your husband to possess? What areas can you work on in your life? How can this serve as a positive example to your husband?
- On a scale of one to ten, how would you rate your level of commitment to God? To your work? To the man in your life? To your family? If single, to the needs of others? How can you increase your score?
- What keeps you from giving your all?
- Do you have unsettled issues that hinder you from being as committed to your relationship with your mate as you should be?

For You Both

When a man and a woman discipline themselves to honor their commitments to each other despite personal feelings or reactions, they will experience the reward of finishing well.

- What is the level of commitment you feel your partner gives to you? to your family? What is their assessment of this question? Discuss this between you.
- How can you help each other bear the cost of your commitments? How can you be more sensitive to each other when the load becomes heavy?
- How can you empower each other to shoulder and balance your responsibilities? How can you pray for each other?
- How can you hold each other accountable without becoming judgmental? Set some game rules.
- In what other ways can you be helpful and encouraging to your spouse?

6

CHARTING THE
RIGHT COURSE

Setting the Stage for Righteousness

But as for me and my household, we will serve the LORD.

JOSHUA 24:15

> The Proverbs 31 man clears the path and leads his wife
> on the course of righteousness.

Women in the world say a good man is hard to find. Women in the
body of Christ say a *godly* man is hard to find. Why is that? I believe,
quiet as this secret is kept, that the heart of a woman searches for
a leader. A priest. A man who will chart a righteous course for her
and her household. Women have a heart that is predisposed to worshiping God and yielding to a man's leadership in matters both spiritual and natural. In return, as helpmeets, they enhance a man's natural
and spiritual lives. Women's inherent sensitivity and spirituality makes

them a natural example for a man to follow into a deeper realm of worship.

At worst, the man who does not stay on track with God loses her respect. At best, he hinders her growth and causes her great sadness. Neither is good. Respect is the foundation of a woman's love for her man. She gives it freely to him if he rises to the occasion and remains uncompromising in his stand for God. Men who don't may feel that a woman who is sold out for God has set a standard too high for them to reach. I am reminded of Sandra Bullock's challenging line to Hugh Grant's character in the movie *Two Weeks Notice.* "It is far easier for you to remain the person you are," she told him, "rather than becoming the man that you should be." Here's another secret: The call a man hears to raise the bar in his life does not come from the woman; it is the still small voice of God. God wants His men to be more than the average man settles for being. God wants him to be a man of godly standards, a man who sets a worthy course for others to follow.

SETTING THE STANDARD

Joshua, Moses' assistant, was unapologetic in his resolute stand for God. After all, he had seen what unbelief and disobedience had cost the nation of Israel. After Moses' death, Joshua assumed command and led God's people into the Promised Land. Years later, when Israel enjoyed a time of peace, Joshua stood before the tribes and urged them to remember the commands of God. He let them know in no uncertain terms that they could live as they chose, but even in the face of their lack of commitment to God, he and his household would go forward with God at the helm (see Joshua 23–24).

Today's culture makes it difficult for a man to stand, but he must. God will empower those who choose Him. Standing alongside Christ, a man can summon the strength to take up his cross daily and die to distractions and temptations that parade before him. He can master the art of self-discipline and be strengthened by God's Word to become an unmovable force in the face of peer pressure. A man has a lot to gain and a lot to lose based on his stand. Think of how many households are destroyed due to a man's infidelity—not just to his wife but to his God as well. Savings are dispersed, homes lost, the family separated, and the children deeply troubled when marital bonds are severed.

> *The man who won't break God's heart can't break his woman's heart because he will already be walking in the right way.*

The Proverbs 31 man is well aware of his own weaknesses and sets firm boundaries that keep him and his woman safe within the confines of Godly conduct. This covers everything from honesty to sex. Any married man will testify that the fight to master lust, for example, doesn't get any easier after you say, "I do." In some cases the temptation gets worse! Men, learn to master discipline before getting married! Consider Joseph: Potiphar's wife stirred up plenty of trouble for him. Double trouble. This beautiful woman *persisted* in propositioning him, this beautiful *married* woman. Could he have gotten away with having an afternoon tryst with her while her husband was away from home? Probably. Was her invitation tempting? He had been sold into slavery and carried far away from home to a foreign land, where he might have had heightened feelings of loneliness and need for love. I would say it was highly likely. Yet in spite of everything pressing in on his flesh, his answer to her was, "How can I do this thing against God?" Joseph did a wise thing: He started avoiding her. He set boundaries for himself in order to stick to his resolve (see Genesis 39).

The married man must strengthen his covenant with his wife to keep himself accountable to her by praying together, worshiping together, believing together, and remaining transparent in his struggles. Together they can set spiritual goals for their mutual growth as well as establish habits that nurture spiritual unity in the home. This discipline is crucial to the health and sustenance of the family. Single women, examine the spiritual and physical discipline of the man you're considering for marriage. What you learn will speak of your future as a couple.

In his lifetime, Moses was the keeper of the Law for the people of Israel. Today, a man is the keeper of the law for his wife and family. The woman is the conduit of worship, setting the atmosphere for prayer and praise. Together they form a unified force, seeking God's face and claiming the victories that come from being in close fellowship with Him. The Proverbs 31 man seeks the heart of God and knows His Word. His care of the woman in his life is not based on her expectations but on God's. The man who won't break God's heart can't break his woman's heart because he will already be walking in the right way—the way of honesty, integrity, faithfulness, and fruitfulness. As Moses lead the children of Israel through the wilderness, a man of God will lead his woman on paths of righteousness in accordance with God's instructions.

Many women have taken over the spiritual leadership in their homes because their husbands have abandoned this post. This is disappointing and frustrating to women. Such abdication leaves them open to the attack of the enemy in the area of discontentment. Small wonder women in many churches practically worship the pastor! He is an example to them of what a man should be. He knows the Word and can get a prayer through to God. How powerful is that in the heart of a woman? It's major—but deadly when the man she esteems so highly takes her husband's place in her heart.

A man's call as priest in his home is to guide his household in the disciplines of being obedient to the Word of the Lord. His prayers will bring fresh manna from heaven when his loved ones need to be fortified with the truth. His prayers will bring water from the rock when his family thirsts for refreshment from God's Spirit.

A MUTUAL CALL TO HOLINESS

The woman who wants to please God wants to do things the right way. If she cannot trust the man she is with to set a standard and keep them both on course, she might, to the frustration of her husband, overcompensate in order to keep herself pure. Her action may in turn cause the man to test her stance by demanding things that could cause her discomfort emotionally, spiritually, or even physically. Any man or woman, in fact, who pushes his or her partner to compromise convictions is not operating in the best interests of that person. Such pressure is a telltale sign of a selfish spirit that does not honor a spouse as it should.

The onus for holiness should not fall entirely on the woman. The Proverbs 31 man knows he has a significant part to play in establishing his family's righteousness. Both partners should be keeping each other in check. When one is weak, the other should be strong and not take advantage of the weakness.

The honor a man receives from his woman will let him know how important this is to her. Singles, look for such complementary strengths in each other; beware of the weaknesses you share. God created partnership to help balance both parties. Let me qualify my confident remarks by saying it takes the right man and the right woman to truly appreciate a godly person. Male or female, those who live a life of compromise will only feel conviction—and might even express disdain—in the presence of someone who values purity. Don't lower your standard. If you've taken a stand for righteousness, the person who does not honor or appreciate your standard is not the partner for you.

CLEARING THE PATH

From dating to courtship to marriage, a man who walks in the light of God's Word clears the path to a deeper love relationship with his

> *A woman longs for a man who will initiate discussion with her about the direction of their lives.*

woman. He is honest about his intentions toward her and is steadfast in godly conduct. Men who do the most effective job of keeping the relationship path clear are those who find a way to stay a step ahead of the relationship. Their stance is offensive rather than defensive. They are clear on what they want, set goals with their partner, and then set the course regarding how they will continue as a couple. Remember, a woman looks for a man who will step up to the plate and be decisive in their life together.

When preparing to go out with a gentleman recently, I started giving him instructions about the plan for the evening. He kindly replied, "Uh, I've taken care of everything already, allow me." Well! He scored ten big points for that. My level of respect for him went waaay up. I relaxed and enjoyed his company and the evening without being distracted by the details.

That is a little thing, but what about the big things such as financial decisions, plans for the future, and daily life as a couple? No man wants to marry his mother, yet she will become one when she feels she is not being taken care of. Unless a man and woman have mutually agreed who is responsible for what in the relationship, the woman should never feel overloaded with responsibilities that her husband simply overlooks or ignores.

What about your spiritual path? Again, the man—the priest, the keeper of the law—should set the course for his household. A woman longs for a man who will initiate discussion with her about the direction of their lives in every area, from choosing a church to having a vision for his family's spiritual growth and well-being. Beyond simply talking about these things, a godly man looks for ways to make the vision a reality, perhaps by establishing time for prayer and study in the family's routines or for other activities that stimulate growth in God. Like Moses, the man is called to be the keeper of the law for his family. When Moses went up Mount Sinai to talk with God, he received the Law—the vision for God's family. But God first confirmed Moses' leadership by coming down and confirming to the people that He was behind Moses. As they walked in obedience together and moved toward a common goal—the Promised Land—all their needs were supplied supernaturally.

Today we know that God has ordained the man to be the leader. Men who do not respond to this important call—setting the course for their household—can lose more than the confidence of their wives. If a man fails to be a champion for righteousness in his home, his losses can be great. I sometimes wonder what type of spiritual leader Jacob was. In chapter 5 we saw that he matured as an honest and responsible man. He knew who God was, and he knew that God was behind the success he experienced. But was he a champion of righteousness? Did he invite his family to participate in his emerging knowledge of God?

When Jacob fled Laban's home, Rachel stole her father's household idols. Laban pursued them, in part to retrieve the idols. Jacob, unaware of Rachel's theft, was so certain they weren't in his possession that he told Laban whoever had the gods would not live. He unwittingly uttered a curse over the head of his most beloved treasure. Laban did not find his gods that day. Rachel hid them and carried them with her, but they did not give the protection she counted on. Rachel died on the way to the Promised Land (see Genesis 31:30-35; 35:16-19).

The spiritual responsibility of a man is a matter of life and death, plain and simple.

The haunting question, of course, is, What was Rachel doing with these gods? Why did she feel the need to have them? Hadn't Jacob taught her to rely on God? Didn't Jacob tell her about the dream he'd had concerning God on the way there? (see Genesis 28:10-22). Hadn't he been consistent in testifying of God's faithfulness and blessing? Hadn't he taken a stand about his belief in God that was crystal clear to his family? Apparently not. Jacob didn't wrestle with God until after Laban left. Whatever compromise remained in Jacob's spirit had to be wrestled out before he could become Israel, the one who strived and prevailed with God.

A very different Jacob raised his son Joseph to be uncompromising in the things of God, but look what he lost first: his favorite wife, the respect of most of his older sons, his good reputation (when his sons went on a murdering spree after the defilement of his only daughter,

Dinah). Even then he lost Joseph, his favorite son, for years because of the blackened hearts of his other sons. When a man does not lay a godly plumb line for his family, the impurity that settles into his household can bring disease and even death, spiritually or physically, to those he loves so dearly. The spiritual responsibility of a man is a matter of life and death, plain and simple. A lack of sound instruction and leadership leaves a family uncovered and open to much pain and heartbreak as they veer without guidance down the wrong path.

Women, if you are willing to settle for an unbelieving man rather than no man at all, the very security of your family will be at stake. Remember, the carnal man cannot comprehend the things of the spirit (see 1 Corinthians 2:14). When you try to share your beliefs, when you try to explain why your children should be raised a certain way, when you try to defend a decision that should be made in accordance with your faith, you will be in trouble. Though a non-Christian man may seem open to such ideas during courtship, he will settle back into who he really is once he has you. The same goes for a man who marries an unsaved woman. Everyone cooperates until they get what they want.

A man who allows himself to be intimidated by a strong woman is no less accountable for the welfare of his family before God. The day of reckoning will come when he will be asked the same question God asked Adam: "Where are you?" The choice is clear-cut: Will you have to live with a woman's resentment or God's disappointment? I dare say the former is easier.

If you are married to a woman who tries to stifle your leadership or wrest it from you, seeking God's face on how to appeal to your wife's heart is essential. There is no pat answer for this situation because each woman is different. Each has her own issues, baggage, needs, and fears.

But God is faithful. Seek Him. He will give you insight into the heart of your wife and disclose why you are being met with resistance. A bridge might need to be mended. A fear that has nothing to do with you and everything to do with her past might be at the root. Whatever it is, God will reveal it and give you instruction on how to lead her. Reaching out to her by encouraging mutual prayer or even a joint Bible study that addresses your issues might help her to hear God's voice on this matter and not just yours. Then her resistance becomes an issue of her obedience to God. Just as I have encouraged women to become the wife their husband wants to cherish, make sure that you are a man your wife wants to submit to. That would be a servant-leader, a loving husband and partner, not a father or a dictator.

MUTUAL SUBMISSION

Just as Moses willingly took responsibility for a people who did not always willingly follow, the Proverbs 31 man is called to be the spiritual leader of his family, setting the dictates of God in motion. The wife who follows the leadership of her husband, though she has her own relationship with God, reaps the benefits of her man's covering and leadership. Submission puts a woman in the position to be provided for, protected, and blessed.

Submission is a rather touchy subject in the church world today. The topic is viewed as sexist, perhaps because the command to submit is nearly always leveled at the woman. The Bible clearly states, however, that we are *all* called to submit to each other (see Ephesians 5:21). How do we balance this theology? By understanding that the woman is not the only one being called to lay down her life.

I first raised the subject of a husband's sacrifice back in chapter 4.

The one who must die to self most in the relationship is the spiritual head. The man is called to love the woman as Christ loved the church and gave His life for it (see Ephesians 5:25). In other words, be willing to sacrifice all, from how you feel to what you want. A husband who loves as Christ does cannot put himself first in the relationship. A true spiritual leader, just as the priests of old who served in the temple, must make sacrifices on behalf of his family.

When God called for a sacrifice, he spoke to Abraham, not Sarah (see Genesis 22). This call was not her responsibility, and so Abraham set off to sacrifice his son Isaac to God. But God stopped Abraham by providing him with a ram (stuck in a nearby bush) to take Isaac's place. The principle we can take away from this story is that the man, as the spiritual head of his household, is called to make sacrifices on behalf of his family. Nowhere does the Bible speak of a woman being asked to die or subject herself to pain for the sake of husband and family. All she is asked to do is submit, which is a dying of sorts, but not to the extreme that laying down one's very life entails.

Submission is easy for a woman who respects her man and trusts him spiritually. I've stated this before, but it bears repeating. When a woman knows her man is well versed in the Word, knowledgeable about the heart of God, and sensitive to His Spirit, she can rest and follow her husband's leadership. Even the strongest woman longs for a man who will be a strong leader. Consider the question the evil queen Jezebel posed to her sullen husband, who had become depressed over not having his way with Naboth's vineyard. "Are you the king of Israel or not?" she asked (1 Kings 21:7, NLT). Every woman longs for a man who would be king, in a sense, over their domain. Otherwise she is driven to feel she must take control over the matters in their home, which can lead to a disastrous outcome in some cases.

A woman seeks a priest for her home. What are the earmarks of a priest? He is the one who not only delivers the law of the Lord to her, but he tenderly washes her in the Word "to make her holy, cleansing her" (Ephesians 5:26). He does not soil her garments with his own compromise. As the spiritual head, his sin can affect his entire household. There is no such thing as a "personal sin"; sin always involves and affects someone else. Though each is responsible to come to God on his or her own, the man in a woman's life assumes the responsibility for her spiritual condition by the example he sets on a daily basis.

The priests of old were also responsible for offering intercessory prayers for God's people. The priest himself had to be sure that he did not come before the Lord in the Holy of Holies bearing any offense himself. He had to wash himself within and without. Specified garments had to be worn. Pure garments.

The modern-day man is called to follow their example of purity. He strives to remain pure in heart and action. He is dressed in robes of righteousness. He does not bear offenses but offers sacrifices continually before the throne room of God. He works at remaining transparent before his wife and God by keeping the family decks clear of sin. Like Job, he is mindful to keep a prayer cover over his family continually. He takes a stand when a stand needs to be taken. He is unapologetic on his godly stance, and yet he is full of mercy and grace. Now that is a man any woman would be willing to follow and imitate.

This is an incredibly tall order for any man! But be encouraged: Remember that you are a work of God in progress, and God delights in the posture of your heart. You don't have to struggle to become a Proverbs 31 man by working solely under the strength of your own efforts. You don't have to find the resources to meet these high expectations within yourself; God will equip you as a member of His family, just as He provided the ram for Abraham. Embrace the family of God around you. Find ways to connect with good men who are striving to walk in the same direction as yourself, and draw from one another's strength, prayers, and encouragement. Good company always makes the journey less arduous. Women do this all the time. For men, the responsibilities are great, and a similar support system is critical in order to stay on course. Remember, you're not alone.

———

The God of Israel spoke, the Rock of Israel said to me:
"When one rules over men in righteousness, when he rules
in the fear of God, he is like the light
of morning at sunrise on a cloudless morning,
like the brightness after rain that brings the grass
from the earth." Is not my house right with God?
Has he not made with me an everlasting covenant,
arranged and secured in every part?
Will he not bring to fruition my salvation
and grant me my every desire?

2 SAMUEL 23:3-5

The Proverbs 31 man lays down his life for his wife
as the ultimate sacrifice unto God.

FOR REFLECTION AND DISCUSSION

For Him

"Praise be to the LORD your God, who has delighted in you and placed you on his throne as king to rule for the LORD your God. Because of the love of your God for Israel and his desire to uphold them forever, he has made you king over them, to maintain justice and righteousness" (2 Chronicles 9:8). "Kings detest wrongdoing, for a throne is established through righteousness" (Proverbs 16:12). "In love a throne will be established; in faithfulness a man will sit on it—one from the house of David—one who in judging seeks justice and speeds the cause of righteousness" (Isaiah 16:5). Walking in righteousness is the first step toward keeping a household on the paths of God. The Proverbs 31 man lovingly leads his family while standing firm in the directions he has been given by God.

- Where are you in your relationship with God? Where do you want it to be?
- What is your prayer life like?
- How do you address being responsible for the spiritual enrichment of the woman in your life? your family?
- What standards for godly living have you set for your household?
- How can you lovingly guide your partner in the path that she should take? How much are you threatened by her spiritual strength?

For Her

"When the righteous thrive, the people rejoice; when the wicked rule, the people groan" (Proverbs 29:2). "The fruit of righteousness will be peace; the effect of righteousness will be quietness and confidence forever" (Isaiah 32:17). A woman must seek a man who maintains a righteous standard of living and nurture this in him by maintaining her own standard for godly living. His leadership will determine the quality of her life, while her lifestyle will affect his leadership.

- How is your relationship with God? What is your prayer life like? Do you compromise your faith because of the man in your life? In what ways?
- If single, what standards have you set as criteria for your future mate?
- If married, where is your husband spiritually? In what ways would you like him to improve? How can you pray for him?
- How much control of your life are you willing to give up to birth godly leadership in the heart of your man by submitting to him?
- How can you partner with him to inspire him to greater levels of faith?

For You Both

Transparent accountability between a man and a woman is key to promoting the trust between them that is needed to establish their mutual submission to each other.

- What responsibilities would you like your mate to assume? How can your partner make you feel secure about taking the lead in these areas?
- How can you contribute to each other's spiritual growth? What are the things that hinder you from moving forward?
- List the unspoken offenses that cause you to abdicate your spiritual responsibility or dig in your heels for more control.
- What do you need to see happening in order to feel you are making progress toward your agreed-upon goals?

7

I'VE GOT YOU COVERED

Protecting Your Woman

"When I looked at you and saw that you were old enough for love,
I spread the corner of my garment over you and covered your nakedness.
I gave you my solemn oath and entered into a covenant with you,"
declares the Sovereign LORD, "and you became mine."

EZEKIEL 16:8

The Proverbs 31 man assumes the responsibility
for covering his wife.

In the above scripture the Lord is speaking to his wife, the nation of Israel. The first thing God does is discern that she is ready and mature enough for love. A man must be critical in his choice of a mate and discern if she is ready for love. How does he discern this? By observation. Is that woman the "good thing" that God has promised? Is she a woman submitted to the instruction of God? Yielded to authority?

Humble in spirit? Seeking the counsel of the Lord and making wise decisions for her life?

Does she, like Ruth, exhibit the capacity to love by serving those who are in need? Is she resourceful, not looking for a handout? Does she demonstrate faithfulness, kindness, and the other traits of mature love set forth in 1 Corinthians 13? Does she display the fruit of the Spirit listed in Galatians 5:22-23? Single ladies, do your homework and see if you are exhibiting these character traits. Ask God to bring you to a place of maturity. Married ladies, you don't get to stop growing after you get your man. God has made a promise to your husband about you—God has told him that you are a good thing who will help to bring more favor to his life—don't make Him a liar!

When God observed His bride and saw that she was ready for love, He was ready to cover her, that is, to be responsible for her care, protection, and provision. He spread the corner of His garment over her, which was a symbolic request for marriage in Old Testament days, and covered her nakedness. He did not wait for her to proclaim her need. He was fully aware of her lack, even if she wasn't. He was not repelled by her needs; rather, he was drawn to them with a committed heart to fulfill them. He took responsibility for shielding her from all to which she was vulnerable in her uncovered state. Just as God delights in our need for Him, a man wants to be needed by the woman in his life. He is drawn to her because he sees a need that he can fill. He will remain by her side if she allows him to do what he was created to. Ladies, don't get confused. Maturity, spiritual or otherwise, does not equal self-sufficiency. On the contrary, maturity frees you to accept, acknowledge, and share your needs with your man or others within your circle of caring.

It is noteworthy that God did not cover His bride entirely. He did not smother or overwhelm her. He covered her just enough to allow freedom of movement on her part. She would have to make a willful choice to stay under that cover in a position to receive His covering; if she ventured too far she would be uncovered. A man should never have to force himself on a woman. By extending himself and his help toward her, he sets the stage for the woman to respond to him and await his mantle.

WHO COVERS WHOM?

What exactly does it mean for a man to cover a woman? Simply this: He takes the responsibility of caring for her needs, protecting her, and ensuring her overall well-being, spiritually, emotionally, and physically.

Just as we have inherited natural genes from our earthly mothers and fathers, we have inherited spiritual genes from our heavenly Father. Just as God has provided covering for all of humankind by sacrificing His own Son Jesus, and Jesus has covered His bride with His own blood, men are called to sacrificially lay down their lives and cover their wives. There's that sacrifice word again! God holds men responsible for this. The prevailing attitude in our Western culture today is "every man for himself; every woman for herself," yet this is not God's point of view.

Though Adam and Eve both fell in the garden after the fruit-eating episode, God homed in on Adam for being at fault. God came looking for *Adam*. He knew if He found Adam that he would locate Eve as well. After all, they were one. God punished them individually, and Adam's chastisement was based on the fact that he had not covered Eve from the wiles of the enemy. He had listened to her and willfully followed her into sin. Through the writings of Paul, Adam's attitude is revealed: "And Adam was not the one deceived; it was the woman who was deceived and became a sinner" (1 Timothy 2:14). In other words, Adam knew better but chose to heed the words of his wife instead of guiding her to follow God's instruction.

It is interesting to me that the woman is not called to cover the man. But a woman can cover *for* a man. She can "have his back," as we say, but having his back is different from being his protection. David was married to Michal, King Saul's daughter. After learning about the demented king's conspiracy to kill David, Michal let David out of the palace window, put an idol in his bed, put goat's hair at the head, and covered it. When the soldiers came to capture David, she told them that he was ill. After discovering that David had escaped, she faced the displeasure of her father, Saul (see 1 Samuel 19:11-17).

> *As a man stands on the foundation of the rock, Christ Jesus, God will cover the man and give him a revelation of Himself, as much as he can handle without being consumed.*

A woman is called to discern the enemies in her husband's life and point them out to him. When she intercedes for him—and sometimes when she intervenes, as Michal did—she empowers her husband to escape the clutches of bondage and even death. Whatever threatens his well-being will be rendered ineffective because of the power of a wise woman's prayers, counsel, or actions. Some might question Michal's loyalty to her husband over her father just as King Saul did, but Michal had a clear understanding of the fact that her first loyalty must be toward her husband (see chapter 4, "Leaving and Cleaving"). When she is covered by him, her loyalty is made secure.

Single women, a special grace from God covers you while you walk alone. God Himself acts as your husband and provides help and provision in supernatural ways, sometimes through godly men. I have heard several of my married friends mention that once they got married, the help they once got from their male family members and friends dwindled significantly. The attitude of these men was, "Your husband should do that for you." And they are right. The baton had been passed. A woman's husband should be her source of help and provision. But for those who have no spiritual covering, God provides.

"Well, who covers the man?" you might ask. The answer is simple —God Himself. When Moses asked God to show him His goodness, God replied, "'I will cause all my goodness to pass in front of you, and I will proclaim my name, the LORD, in your presence. I will have mercy on whom I will have mercy, and I will have compassion on whom I will have compassion. But,' he said, 'you cannot see my face, for no one may see me and live.' Then the LORD said, 'There is a place near me where you may stand on a rock. When my glory passes by, I will put you in a cleft in the rock and cover you with my hand until I have passed by'" (Exodus 33:19-22).

How rich is that? As a man stands on the foundation of the rock (Christ Jesus, see chapter 6), God will cause him to experience His goodness. He will cover the man and give him a revelation of Himself, as much as he can handle without being consumed. In so doing God equipped Moses to do his job, namely, to translate his revelation of the heart of God to the people of Israel. So, too, will God equip His men to do their jobs as priests and protectors of their homes, to bear the Word of the Lord to their households. Then the glory of God will be manifested in a man's home and in the lives of his family.

A PURPOSEFUL HIERARCHY

God has set a hierarchy of authority in place. For the single woman it is God, her father, and then her pastor. For the married woman it is God, her husband, and then her pastor. This authority structure is established to guarantee order and provision for those who submit to it. "Obey your leaders and submit to their authority. They keep watch over you as men who must give an account. Obey them so that their work will be a joy, not a burden, for that would be of no advantage to you" (Hebrews 13:17).

Though many women feel that men in their lives have abused their authority—and many have—this failure must be attributed to human fallacy and not to God's original design. Trusting God, married women must submit to their husbands as unto the Lord. Husbands and wives are included in Scripture's corporate reminder to "be subject to rulers and authorities, to be obedient, to be ready to do whatever is good, to slander no one, to be peaceable and considerate, and to show true humility toward all men" (Titus 3:1-2).

Women, when you strive to take over the role of leader in the relationship, you will suffer because you will be out of order spiritually. It is the responsibility of every man to lovingly keep his wife in spiritual order so that she can reap the full blessings of God in her life.

Covering a woman's weaknesses and insufficiencies is difficult for the man who is willing but meets resistance. Many women today have grown used to doing everything for themselves. They will have to learn how to receive the covering a man offers. Disappointments from broken promises in past relationships make them less trusting of a man who comes bearing good intentions.

Women, when you strive to take over the role of leader in the relationship, you will suffer because you will be out of order spiritually. When you move from beneath the leadership of your husband, you open yourself to the attack of the enemy. The Shulamite woman in Song of Songs 5 did not respond to the call of her husband. Later when she went looking for him after he had withdrawn, the night watchmen found her wandering the streets unprotected. They tore off her veil, struck her, and wounded her. This is a classic example of what happens to the uncovered spouse. When Jezebel decided to take matters into her own hands to get Naboth's vineyard for her husband, her actions ultimately resulted in a curse on her household, loss of the kingdom, and a horrible death. As I mentioned before, men who abdicate their position as leader leave the woman open to the chastisement of God and the consequences of being uncovered. It is the responsibility of every man to lovingly keep his wife in spiritual order so that she can reap the full blessings of God in her life. Remember men, God has your back! A man's instinctive gift of cutting to the chase and embracing the bottom line is a loving guard for the woman, keeping her on track spiritually.

This principle is true for all Christian men, not just husbands. Jesus, as He hung on the cross in the midst of excruciating pain, had the presence of mind to speak these last words to John the beloved concerning His mother, Mary. "When Jesus saw his mother there, and the disciple whom he loved standing nearby, he said to his mother, 'Dear woman, here is your son,' and to the disciple, 'Here is your mother.' From that time on, this disciple took her into his home" (John 19:26-27).

Mary had a husband, though we do not know if he was still alive at this time, as well as other sons, one of them being James (the writer of the book of James). Yet, at the time, Jesus obviously felt that John had

His heartbeat more than the others who followed Him. Jesus would be concerned about not only the physical well-being of his mother but her spiritual well-being, too. Jesus was making sure that Mary would never lack a covering. But I think Jesus was sending a more profound message to men at large. No woman standing before you is just a woman. As a member of the body of Christ, that woman becomes your sister, your mother, and to whatever extent God places her in your life, your responsibility. You *are* your sisters' keeper.

I recall a time early in my Christian life when a group of women at my church got caught up in some teaching that the men did not agree with. All the husbands were opposed. The pastor was adamant that he did not want us attending these meetings any longer. But being the independent women that we were, we ignored their counsel. In our minds, these men just didn't get it! They just weren't *spiritual* enough. So off we went. Oh, the trouble and confusion we encountered as a result! Held captive by false doctrine, it took a great deal of time for us to separate fact from fiction. In retrospect, we all agreed we should have listened to the men. Venturing out from beneath the umbrella of their sound counsel opened us to great spiritual danger and painful consequences.

OPPORTUNITY KNOCKS

So women must learn to acknowledge their need for men in their lives, and men must rise to the occasion, filling the space that God has mandated to them.

Ruth was a woman who had a need for a redeemer. She acknowledged her need for a man like Boaz and made her way to the threshing floor where he slept. Uncovering his feet, she lay down. "In the middle of the night something startled the man, and he turned and discovered a woman lying at his feet. 'Who are you?' he asked. 'I am your servant Ruth,' she said. 'Spread the corner of your garment over me, since you are a kinsman-redeemer'" (Ruth 3:8-9). What was she saying to him? "I need your protection and provision!" Boaz was a member of her dead husband's family lineage. According to cultural practices of the time, he was responsible for her well-being. Ruth was clearly an able woman. She had walked her mother-in-law all the way back from Moab and had found a way to provide sustenance for them. Even so, she was not ignorant of her limitations and willingly admitted them. In those days, a woman alone lived a hard life and depended on the kindness of strangers. Doesn't sound much different from modern times, does it? She was at risk of being taken advantage of on many levels. She needed a redeemer. She needed the protection and assistance of a man. She needed his presence in her life.

> Covering a woman's heart and mind as well as her body is part of what is required to ensure her security and release her to serve her husband without fear or reticence.

Ruth not only submitted her need to Boaz, she reminded him of his obligation as a member of the family. Many women today are not even aware of the responsibility a man has toward them, so they do not challenge a man to step up to the plate. They do not make a man responsible for their hearts and well-being. They walk with guarded hearts and seek their own provision. When a woman does this, her man is more likely to think she's "got it covered" and is not as sensitive as he should be to her needs. As a result, everyone internalizes their struggle with the other, and the relationship is fractured.

Men, let's be clear: You cannot wait for a woman's direction in this matter. God holds you responsible for covering your woman's heart, mind, body, and soul. Lovingly ask her to share her needs with you and be willing to discuss them. Ask God to show you the unapparent sensitivities and weaknesses of the woman in your life. Ask Him to equip you to provide for her with wisdom and grace. Then do all you can to protect and care for those vulnerable places.

In an old episode of *All in the Family*, the husband and wife, Mike and Gloria, have an argument over who should be responsible for contraception. Mike says to Gloria, "Well, the woman is the one with all the parts that need to be protected!" Gloria shoots back, "Oh yeah? Well the man has all the parts a woman needs to be protected from!" You might say that exchange mirrors the sentiments of a lot of women who have grown leery of trusting a man with their hearts or their lives. Yet they must trust their hearts to God and release the things they hold closely as that man earns their trust. This is part of being mature enough for love. And yes, a man must earn that trust through the consistency of his actions toward his woman, which should reflect the care and consideration he has for her. Later in that episode, after much discussion and a mutual agreement, Mike decides to get a vasectomy. I am not advocating this as something every man should run out and do. His decision is simply a good illustration of a sacrifice this particular husband was willing to make to cover his wife and give her the security she needed. Covering a woman's heart and mind as well as her body is part of what is required to ensure her security and release her to serve her husband without fear or reticence.

The difference a man makes in a woman's world is unspeakable. What would Mary, the mother of Jesus, have done without Joseph? The angel visited Joseph, the leader of the house, and gave him this urgent news: Herod planned to murder every boy-child in the region. He must leave immediately and take his family to Egypt. Joseph sprang into action, packed up his new family, and escorted them safely to Egypt and back at the appointed time. Notice again who received the instruction and carried out the mission.

What would Esther have done without the assistance of her king? Upon hearing of the evil plot of Haman against the people of Israel, Esther did not take up arms herself or solve the problem alone. Instead, she prepared to go to her husband and plead for his intervention. Sometimes when a man is focused on making a living for his family, he is not as aware of issues that might arise in his household. A woman often has the unique gift of being sensitive to the areas a man over-looks. As she brings these things to her husband's attention, he is called to respond to them accordingly.

After serving the king several meals, Esther presented her dilemma. Upon hearing her predicament, the king sprang into action. Anything that affected the welfare of his queen affected him. He took her problem personally, as he should. But there was one hitch. The king himself had set her problem in motion. He was the one who had signed off on the attack against the Jews. But that did not hinder him from finding a solution. He superimposed another law on top of the edict he had issued and gave the Jews the right to defend themselves. There is an answer for every quandary if one is creative enough to find it. Sometimes the situations of life cannot be changed—they are what they are. At times like these, a man's resourcefulness is tested. In this case, the king's solution worked. The Jews slaughtered their enemies and put them to flight. Afterward, the king returned to Esther to give her a full report of what had happened and to ask her what else she needed.

The Proverbs 31 man, once apprised of any situation, responds to the need. He sees his mission through to the end, thereby securing victory for his household.

In 1 Samuel 30 we see David returning home from battle to find that his two wives had been kidnapped along with all the women and children in his camp. As the men despaired, David sought the Lord. He did not give into self-pity or resignation; he asked the Lord for direction, and then he went off in hot pursuit of what belonged to him. David didn't fight to protect his ego; he fought to protect what he loved. He could not leave his women in a dangerous situation to be defiled and used by those who did not know the priceless treasure they had. No, he must rescue them from harm's way and preserve their lives. He hesitated only long enough to ask God what to do, and then he was off to the races with God as his partner. He pursued the enemy, found them, slayed them, and reclaimed his two brides, along with everything else that had been stolen.

> *Establishing the security of a woman is not something a man can do without the assistance of God. Only through God's instruction can a man become effective in this endeavor.*

Today, more men abdicate than fight, except in the movies. It is a rare man who will not give up in his pursuit of his bride before or after the marriage. Yet this pursuit is what solidifies in a woman's mind that she is valuable to her man (more on this in chapter 9). Whatever is worth having is worth fighting for.

Establishing the security of a woman is not something a man can do without the assistance of God. God, who knows her state of mind, the condition of her heart, and her secret fears and insecurities, is more than willing to tell the man in her life how to help her war against the enemies of her soul. Only through God's instruction can a man become effective in this endeavor. To march into battle without God will only lead to frustration and feelings of defeat. The God who gives insight will make a man's way easier as he seeks to do the things needed to build a fortress of security around his woman's heart.

WHEN A MAN WITHHOLDS HIS PROTECTION

A woman can help a man who wants to protect her by covering him with prayer. Asking God to speak to his heart and make him sensitive to the voice of the Holy Spirit who will reveal your needs. Women are very vocal and great communicators—sometimes "too great" for a man to handle. Sometimes a woman can drown out the voice of the Holy Spirit, who is trying to deal with the man. Learn to pick wisely what you share and how often you share. Don't be ruled by your emotions or the need to make him understand you.

Abigail, who was married to the fool Nabal, did not spend a lot of time trying to tell Nabal his faults. She trusted God. When Nabal refused to cover his family, leaving them open to death at the hands of King David, God removed him, and struck him dead in his own home (see 1 Samuel 25). This is a rather harsh measure of discipline, but God must have deemed it necessary. God will not allow a man to remain in the life of a good woman and not take the appropriate steps to secure her welfare. He won't physically kill them all, but he will deal with them in tangible ways. There are serious consequences for foolish men who refuse to live up to their God-ordained position in a marriage. Where that man fails, God will fill in the gap for the woman. The man, however, will not escape his correction, for the fool within him must die in order for the king—what he was designed to be—to live in the fullness of his calling.

Lot, who chose to live in Sodom after parting ways with Abraham, found himself and his household kidnapped and plundered when the enemies of the region attacked these cities. Upon learning of Lot's plight, Abraham mobilized the men of his household, chased after the army, and saved Lot, his family, and possessions, including the women and other captives. But what did Lot do? He took his family right back to where they had been living! He knew the city was a corrupt and wicked society, yet he did not protect his family by removing them. Later we find Lot having to be rescued from the same city by angels sent from God in answer to Abraham's prayer. In flight, Lot loses his wife as she looks back to catch a last glimpse of home and is turned into a pillar of salt. Apparently, after all is said and done, we each have to be responsible before God for the decisions we make.

If only Lot had made different decisions concerning his wife and family! Who knows why they moved back to Sodom. Perhaps Lot's wife insisted she was not going to leave their beautiful home to strangers after working so hard to build it. Even if that was the case, Lot would be held responsible for this final decision. It seems that he was not a very strong man. After begging the angels to allow him to settle in a spot he selected rather than fleeing Sodom for the place they had told him to go to, he allowed his own daughters to get him drunk and seduce him, impregnating them both. The offspring of these children grew up to become enemies of Israel. Talk about ruining his legacy. Proverbs 13:22 says, "A good man leaves an inheritance for his children's children," but all Lot left were the consequences of numerous bad choices.

LAYING DOWN THE LAW

Moses' sister, Miriam, led worship for the people of Israel. This was an important position, but Moses was the appointed head. When Miriam and Aaron spoke against Moses for marrying an Ethiopian woman and considered rejecting his authority, saying, "Doesn't God speak to us also?" the Lord descended in the form of a cloud, and His anger burned against them. The Lord said to Miriam and Aaron: "Listen to my words: When a prophet of the LORD is among you, I reveal myself to him in visions, I speak to him in dreams. But this is not true of my servant Moses; he is faithful in all my house. With him I speak face to face, clearly and not in riddles; he sees the form of the LORD. Why then were you not afraid to speak against my servant Moses?" (Numbers 12:6-8). When the cloud of the Lord lifted, Miriam was leprous.

Isn't it interesting that Aaron was not? Aaron was called to be a priest; he was considered an overseer of the camp as well as Moses. As a priest he could not be unclean. God needs His men to be clean inside and out in order to effectively lead His women. But Miriam, though she was a worship leader, was still called to be under the authority of Moses. Moses then had to intercede for Miriam and ask God not to punish her. After Moses sought God on her behalf, God forgave her. It was Moses' continual seeking of God's will for the people's lives, in fact, that led them from the wilderness to the Promised Land.

> *Submission is borne out of trust because the actions of the man reflect his intentions for his wife's welfare. The respect she pays her husband strengthens him to stand as he should as a faithful cover.*

Within God's design, as the man covers the woman, she willingly submits. Submission, as I mentioned in chapter 6, is borne out of trust because the actions of the man reflect his intentions for her welfare. The respect she pays her husband strengthens him to stand as he should as a faithful cover. In turn, the weaknesses of the woman are compensated for in the strength of the man and vice versa. The weaknesses of both are compensated for by God. Together they form a unified strong unit that can stand the test of trial and storms, covering each other in an embrace that cannot be broken.

> A man ought not to cover his head, since he is the image and glory of God; but the woman is the glory of man. For man did not come from woman, but woman from man; neither was man created for woman, but woman for man. For this reason, and because of the angels, the woman ought to have a sign of authority on her head.
>
> In the Lord, however, woman is not independent of man, nor is man independent of woman. For as woman came from man, so also man is born of woman. But everything comes from God. (1 Corinthians 11:7-12)

There you have it. All rights to authority come from God. As man receives his covering, he extends that covering over his wife. That covering is significant of the presence, power, authority, and provision of God, which is His glory. When a man is on his job, it is reflected in his wife and household. Order and stability are made apparent in their lives. The body is a reflection of the head, and no member is independent from the other. When the head suffers, the rest of the body suffers with it. This is why God says that the man and woman are not independent of each other. So God covers the man. The man covers the woman. Together they cover their children. Together His glory is manifested in their lives as a testimony of the presence and goodness of God in their midst.

As a tree spreads its branches and covers that which sits beneath its shade, so a man is called to cover his wife and household and bear fruit in season and out of season, regardless of the elements at work. The roots of such a prosperous tree dig deep into the living water of God's Word to sustain itself in dry weather and continue to stand immovable (see Psalm 1:3).

God is man's source of refreshment during times of dryness in his relationship with his wife. A husband who taps into the presence of God will find rivers of living water in Him. God will provide the resources he needs to yield to the growth that God requires and to be fruitful to the glory of God even through adverse conditions. Again, for those who do not grow weary of doing good, in due season they will reap a rich harvest—not just enough to feed themselves but an abundance that will benefit others as well.

———

*Husbands, in the same way be considerate as you live
with your wives, and treat them with respect as the weaker
partner and as heirs with you of the gracious gift of life,
so that nothing will hinder your prayers.*

1 PETER 3:7

*The Proverbs 31 man recognizes the needs of his wife
as an opportunity to bless her.*

FOR REFLECTION AND DISCUSSION

For Him

"Now I want you to realize that the head of every man is Christ, and the head of the woman is man, and the head of Christ is God" (1 Corinthians 11:3). "For the husband is the head of the wife as Christ is the head of the church, his body, of which he is the Savior" (Ephesians 5:23). Man is the God-appointed representative of Christ in the earth. He is called to yield to the authority of God and use the authority given him by God to care for his wife in love.

- How do you feel about submitting to the authority of God? How do you feel about serving your wife?
- How much do you give of yourself to your woman? How much do you receive? Would you say the exchange is 100/100 or a lesser fraction?
- In what ways do you protect and provide for the woman in your life? What do you do to make her feel secure physically, spiritually, and emotionally?
- How do you cultivate her trust in you?
- Do you have her respect? If no, why not? What steps can you take to gain trust and respect from her?

For Her

"Wives, submit to your husbands, as is fitting in the Lord" (Colossians 3:18). "A wife of noble character is her husband's crown, but a disgraceful wife is like decay in his bones" (Proverbs 12:4). A woman has a lot of bearing on her husband's reputation. The qualities you possess speak volumes to his peers. The respect you show him will inspire those around him to respect him as well.

- Do you have a problem with submission? What is at the heart of your struggle? How could relying on God help you entrust yourself to your man?
- Do you have difficulty trusting men? What experience led to this?
- What do you need from your mate to feel secure?
- Are you able to vocalize your needs to your husband or significant other? What is your expectation after you have expressed your needs? Is what you desire realistic and in alignment with God's Word?
- How can you cultivate his sensitivity to your needs?

For You Both

As partners you are called to submit one to the other; it is in the yielding that both find their needs met above measure.

- Is your mate sensitive to your needs? What is your response?
- How can you foster an atmosphere that lends itself to honesty and vulnerability between the two of you?
- Do you confront your spouse or lovingly share from your heart? Do you give each other permission to fail? What hinders you from doing so? What agreement can you make to help facilitate more grace in your relationship?
- How can you restore each other after a disappointment?
- What do you need from your mate to make you feel secure? What walls do you need to remove from around your heart in order for your relationship to grow stronger?

8

THE PRICE OF A RING

Valuing the Marriage Covenant

Suppose one of you wants to build a tower. Will he not first sit down
and estimate the cost to see if he has enough money to complete it?

LUKE 14:28

The Proverbs 31 man realizes that his word equals his life
and makes the sacrifice needed to honor his vows.

Most women love jewelry. Lots of time, investigation, and speculation
go into a woman's dreams of her engagement and wedding ring. Everyone has a picture in her own mind of what it looks like, how big the
diamond will be, and the oohs and aahs of admiration she will receive
when she proudly displays this much-coveted gift from her beloved.
Not many consider the cost. Well, the man does, since he has to pay for
it! But just as the price of a wedding does not equal the cost of a marriage, the price of the ring does not equal the true cost of the covenant
it represents.

Though modern tradition says a ring should cost a man three months of his income, from God's viewpoint that ring should cost him his very life. With it he makes a vow to love his wife in sickness and in health, for richer or for poorer, forever and ever amen. What does that really mean in lay terms? That love for his wife must be cultivated and sustained no matter what. Back in days of old, a ring was more than just an accessory. Men wore signet rings for business purposes and used them to imprint seals on agreements and contracts. When the king applied his seal to any document, the conditions of what were written in it could not be altered or revoked. His stamp of approval was binding forever. Similarly, under the binding covenant of marriage, "I do" means forever. A Proverbs 31 man perseveres through the hard times, finds a way to work things out, and sticks with the plan until he and his wife make it through the storm.

Wedding vows leave out a lot of the specific troubles that threaten a marriage. Some are as trivial as weight gain or as tragic as adultery or the death of a child. Perhaps the traditional vows should be expanded to include a list of things that can rock the foundation of a marriage. Perhaps, in considering the broad scope of events that could occur, people would think twice before saying "I do." On the other hand, perhaps the overwhelming nature of the possibilities is best left unsaid. No one plans for difficulty to interrupt the bliss they feel in this wonderful season, and yet life inevitably happens to the best of couples. How they weather the trials speaks volumes of their character and commitment to each other.

The words a couple utters at the altar are spiritual; therefore, they have life.

In the midst of trouble, our emotions put our vows at risk. God takes vows very seriously, however, and expects us to control what we do with our feelings. King Solomon learned this and warned, "Do not let your mouth lead you into sin. And do not protest to the temple messenger, 'My vow was a mistake.' Why should God be angry at what you say and destroy the work of your hands?" (Ecclesiastes 5:6).

All that a man and woman have worked for can be wiped out when circumstances cause them to forget their vows. It is sin to make a promise and then break it! The disappointment that one feels if a courtship is broken cannot compare to the pain of brokenness experienced by two people who have entered into a covenant to be a part of each other's lives till death do they part.

Of Contracts and Covenants

The words a couple utters at the altar are spiritual; therefore, they have life. Marriage vows graft the spirits of two people together in a bond of unity. With God as the third cord binding them together and strengthening them, that bond cannot be easily broken. A severed bond always affects more than the two people involved. Children struggle with their own identity and loyalties or believe they are the reason for the separation of their parents. Friends fear they will be asked to pick sides. Parents are saddened as they witness the pain of their adult children. The ripple effect is lifelong and reaches well beyond the actual divorce. The kingdom of God also suffers, as each shattered marriage weakens our witness to the world. Small wonder God expects everyone to keep the vows they make in the presence of witnesses.

Today couples sign marriage contracts. Some add prenuptial agreements to insure themselves against loss should the union disintegrate. But God does not plan on ever severing His commitment to His bride—the corporate body of believers. He's in this thing for eternity. The attitude at the heart of this kind of commitment is what distinguishes the covenant from the contract. You see, most contracts are conditional. For example, "I'll fulfill my end of the bargain *if* you do this or that. I don't have to live up to the end of my deal if you don't live up to yours." Or, "You must fulfill your part of the commitment within a specified time period, or the agreement is off!"

Covenant doesn't work like that. Covenant is not based on time or conditions. It operates on the principle of grace. In spite of what one party does or does not do, the agreement still stands. The one who made the covenant continues to walk in it. God designed the union between a man and woman to be bound by an unbreakable covenant, not a conditional contract as so many are today. In marriage, a man must understand the ramifications of the covenant promises he makes to a woman. He must be a man of covenant. I'll say it again: Covenants are not broken. To break an oath or a promise is to shatter the spirit of the one who laid claim to it. Therefore, think before you or your actions "speak," and then speak carefully. God takes every idle word into account. Ladies, the same truth applies to you as well.

A promise is a promise to the Lord. It has no end. And He seals this promise with blood. God made a promise to Abraham concerning the lineage of people that would spring from his bloodline. He sealed His promise by passing through the body of several animals that had been cut in half (see Genesis 15:17). Men of old imitated this rite through a "blood brothers" pact signifying, "If I don't keep my promise to you, may I be considered as dead as the carcass before you." A covenant then was a life-and-death commitment, as it still should be. As the bride and groom now say today, "Till death do us part."

God's covenant with His people was ultimately sealed with the blood of Jesus. Jesus literally drew a line of blood between us and the devil, which Satan cannot cross. Then He grafted us into His family tree, and we became a part of His bloodline (see Romans 11:17-19 and Ephesians 2:12-13). We became His possession just as He had promised His bride initially. In Jewish tradition of the past, as well as in many Third-World countries, when a man took a woman to be his wife, their covenant was sealed by the blood of her virginity being shed on the wedding night. Today, amid shifting morals, this tradition is no longer widely observed. In the eyes of God, however, a man's commitment to the woman still bears tremendous weight, and God will hold him responsible for the life of the covenant he has made to his bride. God hates divorce (see Malachi 2:16) because the severing of the covenant will always bring death—a death from which He wants to save us. As human beings, when we yield to our fleshly desires instead of God's commands, we will not be able to stand the test of time, trials, and disappointments. For this reason God covered our entrance fee to the heavenly wedding feast He has planned for us with the blood of His own Son. In this way, His covenant with us will endure forever, so that no matter what, we will be able to enter into the fullness of His promise.

In a world of instant gratification, men and women alike prefer—perhaps even expect—instant remedies for their troubles, but that is not the reality of life. Spectacular victories will be given, however, to those who fight with their lives to honor their covenants.

LITMUS TEST

There is a season (perhaps there are many) in every romance when love will be tested. A wise old woman once told me that a man has to go through some obstacle to get the woman he wants, or it will never be evident to him how much he desires her. A difficulty will present itself that tests his love for her. A Proverbs 31 man will do everything he can to make it past that barrier so he will not be robbed of the one he desires.

A man needs to know what is in a woman's heart before committing to her and vice versa. How important is each to the other?

> *Pay attention to what you learn about each other during trials in your relationship before marriage; chances are those revelations will hold true after you say your vows as well.*

What is the likelihood that this person will honor his or her vows after the wedding? Even the Lord does this with us. When His bride, the Israelites, were wandering in the wilderness, Moses reminded them, "Remember how the LORD your God led you all the way in the desert these forty years, to humble you and to test you in order to know what was in your heart, whether or not you would keep his commands" (Deuteronomy 8:2). Pay attention to what you learn about each other during trials in your relationship before marriage. Chances are those revelations will hold true after you say your wedding vows as well.

The song goes that when a man loves a woman he'll trade the world for the good thing he's found. The price of a ring is one thing. The cost of love is another. Love costs you everything—your pride, your priorities, yourself. Therefore, love is worthy of discernment. Any investor fully researches the value of his investment before committing to it. But upon finding that it has great value, he is willing to give his all to acquire it, knowing the returns will far surpass the initial investment.

Psalm 16:11 speaks of eternal pleasures being found at the right hand of God. In the Greek Orthodox tradition, the bride and groom still wear their rings on the right hand to signify blessings on their union. The blessings bestowed on a couple that has been discerning before marriage are indeed a rich return.

A Covenant-Honoring Pursuit

A Proverbs 31 man makes a choice to honor his covenant with his wife even before their wedding. Such acknowledgment of the marriage covenant's importance even before it is formalized sets a man apart. His honoring actions begin with his attitude toward the pursuit of his woman. His attitude is a good indicator of what a woman can expect after the ceremony. She would not go wrong in using it as a key factor in deciding whether to spend the rest of her life with this man.

I have watched men in amazement as they go through all kinds of gyrations to capture the heart of the woman they want. Even looking back through the Word, David comes to mind. In order to win the hand of King Saul's daughter Michal, David had to kill one hundred Philistines and present their foreskins to Saul. The king was hoping David would be killed, but David succeeded and returned with *two* hundred foreskins! He went the extra mile to win the hand of Michal fair and square. (Later Michal messed up the marriage by her own actions, but don't think she wasn't considered a prize until then.)

One of my favorite television shows used to be *Family Matters,* a cute little sitcom that largely focused on the attempts of a gangly nerd named Urkle to win the affections of his beloved Laura. Outwardly speaking, he was not the kind of guy Laura had in mind. I recall one particular episode when the school hunk—a gorgeous star athlete and heartthrob—asks Laura out. This truly upsets Urkle, who challenges the guy in gym class to a contest of strength and quickness on the rope climb. Needless to say, he fails miserably. Embarrassed and disappointed, Urkle vows to win the following week. As he makes pathetic attempts to build his muscles before the contest day, Laura tells him she is surprised at how he has handled the situation. She explains that the one thing she appreciates about him is his intelligence, and she urges him to stick to what he does best. When the day of the rematch finally comes, Urkle arrives strapped into a device that he has invented. It shoots him to the top of the rope and back down in seconds. He wins the hand of his heart's desire—the lovely Laura.

> The man who responds to God's design by pursuing the woman he loves will be more likely to honor his responsibilities to run his household within the covenant of marriage.

Urkle might not have been the hunk that every woman dreams of, but his heart and mind made up for what his teenage body lacked. His persistence hinted at the real man that he would eventually become and also made Laura consider how superficial she had been.

Real men capitalize on their best attributes and do whatever is necessary to win the heart of the woman they want. My own dad spotted my mother and pursued her. She wasn't interested, said he wasn't her type. That didn't stop him; he was a man on a mission! He wooed her with presents and kindness and sweet actions that finally won her heart, and here I am today.

Some would say that men in pursuit reflect an old-school way of thinking. It just doesn't go that way anymore. Today men are passive and women are the aggressors. To some extent this is true, but not across the board. In any case, if the woman is the aggressor in the relationship, it is seriously out of order (see chapter 7). A man should not allow his ego to deceive him and lead him into a relationship he may regret later. The Bible is clear that *he* who finds a wife finds a good thing and obtains favor (see Proverbs 18:22), not the other way around. The enemy has stripped many men in church of their sexuality by making them view their natural response to attraction as unholy. Yet God created men to be moved by what they see. This deception has shut down men in the church and rendered them fearful of approaching women. The lack of pursuit from men is fueling the desperation of women in the church. Let me set you free, men: If you see a woman you like, it is all right to approach her, be friendly, you know…go for it!

Men go hunting for what they want. The heart of the conqueror that God put within them gains pleasure in the pursuit. I believe that men who are caught by women still have the need to be engaged in a hunt. Perhaps this explains why some men's hearts wander after marrying a woman who pursued them. Men, if you're flattered when a woman pursues you, consider this: The woman is already running the relationship, and she will have a hard time submitting to you in marriage. Women, consider the possibility that a man who is passive in his pursuit of you will likely be passive later in other areas that are important to you. The bottom line is that he either will not be interested or will lack significant drive to follow through to other achievements. The man who responds to God's design by pursuing the woman he loves will be more likely to honor his responsibilities to run his household within the covenant of marriage.

Some speculate that "the lover" and "the beloved" of Song of Songs are King Solomon and Abishag, the young virgin who warmed King David's bed in his last days (see 1 Kings 1–2). After David died, she returned to her village, and Solomon went in hot pursuit to claim her as his bride. As she stood working in the fields, the king's chariots overtook her, and he declared his love for her. She must have felt like the most beautiful woman on the planet by the time he was finished listing all of her attributes! (See Song of Songs 4.) She was moved by his words of praise and fell deeply in love with him.

The Proverbs 31 man is a discriminating man and an intentional man. He makes a plan for his life, charts his course, and keeps God's purpose for him in mind when evaluating who would be a good partner for his life (see chapter 2). He honors the value of a woman's heart by honestly communicating his intentions and expectations throughout their friendship. He does not waste a woman's time simply to have company. Experimenting with a woman's heart is unacceptable and should not happen.

If a man sees a woman in his life as only a friend, that should be clear, and his signals toward her should never be mixed. Friendship entails walking together in transparency and accountability, learning about each other, sharing common interests, and enjoying each other's company without any expectations apart from the basic considerations. If he is not clear about how he feels, he should say so. Then the woman can make a choice at her own risk whether to proceed.

If a man is interested in courtship, he should make his intentions clear and be responsible for setting the relationship on track as well as leading it. Courtship is a time of cultivating a relationship with the intention of heading toward marriage. It is a time of giving, sharing, and learning more about the needs of your intended. It is a time to grow in transparency and accountability toward each other and a time to make plans for the future. Sometimes a woman needs to be won, but this challenge does not deter him. He seeks God in prayer to find out the way to her heart (see chapter 7) and then proceeds until he wins it. Anything worth having is worth fighting for.

HONOR AND PURITY

Though the world tells men that the true measure of their manhood is how many women they can sleep with, that is not God's measure of a man. God considers women to be valuable commodities. Perhaps that is the heart of a father. I had a conversation with a friend recently about his three-year-old daughter. He said to me, "I never knew girls were so special. Perhaps I would have been better." When I asked what he meant, he answered, "I wouldn't have been so abusive. I just didn't know. I was trying to figure it out for myself and hurt many women in the process." If parents don't raise sons to understand how precious women are, these valuable jewels will never get the appreciation they deserve.

God has reserved sexual intimacy for the marriage bed because it is the seal of the covenant that a man and woman make between them. It is a ministry one to the other that refreshes their love for each other and binds them together in a way that words cannot. In God's eyes, the woman is like the Holy of Holies. She is a place to be entered bearing no offense, only reverence, love, and honor. The man is a type of high priest, who goes into the Holy of Holies pure of heart and spirit and ministers to his beloved. The woman responds, and the couple is blessed. When the priest of old presented offerings and went into the Holy of Holies to worship God, the glory of God filled that place. They were consumed with His presence. It was a powerful exchange between man and God. In the same way, sexual intimacy is a powerful experience between a man and a woman. It should be free of angst, doubt, and fear of what the morning will bring—distractions that are typically present in the absence of a commitment.

A man is called to protect a woman, whether she is his wife or not (see chapter 7). Men and women alike must know that God holds the man responsible for securing the heart of a woman in a godly, binding commitment before expecting to exchange intimacy. If a man knows he has no plans to make the woman before him his wife, he should protect her heart by not touching her body. For those who do plan to marry the woman in their life, this is the rule until after *the marriage ceremony,* not until after you have both agreed to be engaged. Anything can happen before the wedding day.

Honoring the marriage bed before marriage builds a foundation of trust that will last throughout the marriage. A man will never wonder if his wife would sleep with another man if she would not sleep with him before their wedding night. He will rest secure in the knowledge that she is a woman who lives by godly principle, exercising self-control. Self-control is something you prove to your mate *before* marriage, not after.

The brothers of the Shulamite woman Abishag questioned her on her virginity, wanting to know if she had kept herself pure while in the palace of David. Had she been a "door" allowing men to enter her rather than a "wall" keeping them away from her intimately? If so, they would punish her with death. But if she had kept her chastity, they would heap her with honor. She was able to proudly reply that she was a "wall," and as the Knox translation says, "impregnable this breast as a fortress; and the man who claimed me found in me a bringer of content" (Song of Songs 8:10). In other words, because I have kept myself pure, the man in my life knows I am a woman of substance who can be trusted, and this gives him peace of mind!

This same woman, though sick with love, offered very good insight to her other friends. "Daughters of Jerusalem, I charge you by the gazelles and by the does of the field: Do not arouse or awaken love until it so desires" (Song of Songs 2:7). In other words, there is no need to rush; allow love to take its rightful course. In God's perfect order, the time for sexual intimacy is the wedding night.

As I've mentioned before, many men have a tendency to take a woman's stand on purity as a personal rejection. A man needs to have a clear understanding that a woman's decision to walk according to the Word of God has nothing, yet everything, to do with him. First, that woman wants to be pleasing to God above all things. A Proverbs 31 man wants to help her achieve this worthy goal. Second, she honors that man too much to reduce sex with him to something that is not sacred and special. Outside of marriage, sex is nothing more than an act or a lie. It speaks of promises it cannot keep. Inside of marriage, it is a truthful response to love through giving.

KEEPING YOUR VOWS AFTER MARRIAGE

Many might be thinking, *Boy I sure missed it. I did not take the time to be as discerning as you suggest before I married my mate. What do I do now, Michelle?* Do not despair. Keep hope alive. The wonderful thing about God's grace is it was invented to cover our mistakes as well as the difficult places in our lives. (Remember God as the center on the basketball court of our lives?) But grace does much more. It gives us a new beginning. First of all, return to your first love. What was it about your spouse that made you want to spend the rest of your life with him or her in the first place? Obviously, this person possessed desirable qualities that might have been diminished by other issues that cropped up after your wedding. Needless to say, your partner might bear the same mind-set toward you! Now is the time to make an important decision to honor the covenant you've made. Go back and do the things you used to do to cultivate love between you. Renew your vows to each other. In return, God will honor you. He will equip you with the grace to love and be in love with your partner. He will open your heart and fill it with His love for your mate and bring restoration to every part of your life. Because ultimately, your entire life will be affected according to how you honor or dishonor the covenant you've made with your spouse. In Malachi 2:13-15, God chastises those who have broken a covenant by saying:

> You flood the LORD's altar with tears. You weep and wail because
> he no longer pays attention to your offerings or accepts them
> with pleasure from your hands. You ask, "Why?" It is because the
> LORD is acting as the witness between you and the wife of your
> youth, because you have broken faith with her, though she is
> your partner, the wife of your marriage covenant.
>
> Has not the LORD made them one? In flesh and spirit they
> are his. And why one? Because he was seeking godly offspring. So
> guard yourself in your spirit, and do not break faith with the wife
> of your youth.

"Guard yourself in your spirit!" That's good. The war against marriage begins in the mind before it takes root in the flesh. You've all heard that love is not a feeling, it is a decision. When your decision is being tested, submit yourself to God and allow Him to strengthen your resolve to persevere.

Remember, in the midst of relationship trials, the trouble is never all about the other person. God will use the situation to grow sweeter fruit in you as well. And finally, don't break faith with the wife (or husband) of your youth. Consciously shattering a relationship is comparable to rupturing that person's faith. The faith they put in you as well as in God. Both relationships are on the line. Give your spouse a reason to trust and hope in you as well as in God's restorative power, again by persisting in love until you reach a breakthrough. As I said early in this chapter, there is no expiration date on a covenant. It is binding until the end, and no matter how long it takes, Christ's grace will continu-

> *One of the first words a child learns to say is "mine!" But true maturity is walking with open hands and being willing to say "ours" or, if need be, simply "yours."*

ally work in us to reconcile us with our first love. All we have to do is yield and cooperate with His Spirit who is at work within us.

WHEN A MAN LOVES A WOMAN

In a marriage, one's life is no longer "I" but "we." Concessions have to be made for the benefit of the other person. Failure to do so calls love into question. Each partner must learn to give and take in order to balance the relationship and move toward becoming one in spirit. Self must die, as selfishness cannot coexist with mature love. Being "in love" is about how the other person makes you feel, but loving is about how *you* make the *other* person feel.

"God so loved the world that he gave..." He gave his most precious possession—His very own Son—as a ransom to gain His bride. He washed her in His Word. He dressed her in robes of righteousness and crowned her His first priority. He forgives...and forgives again. He constantly reaches out to her when she strays and forever seeks reconciliation. He constantly woos her to His side and shields her from her enemies. He maintains her purity until the wedding day and prepares a place for her. Love is costly even to God, but it is a price He will gladly pay.

One of the first words a child learns to say is "mine!" But true maturity is walking with open hands and being willing to say "ours" or, if need be, simply "yours."

———

"Seal it with the king's signet ring—
for no document written in the king's name
and sealed with his ring can be revoked."

ESTHER 8:8

The Proverbs 31 man considers the cost of a commitment to the woman in his life and pays it.

FOR REFLECTION AND DISCUSSION

For Him

"What a man [or woman] desires is unfailing love; better to be poor than a liar" (Proverbs 19:22). "Greater love has no one than this, that he lay down his life for his friends" (John 15:13). "An unmarried man is concerned about the Lord's affairs—how he can please the Lord. But a married man is concerned about the affairs of this world—how he can please his wife—and his interests are divided" (1 Corinthians 7:32-34). A man must make the decision to love the woman in his life purely and sacrificially. It is in the laying down of his life for his wife that he reaps abundant rewards and the fulfillment he desires.

- What does the picture of your family look like when you envision it? How will you facilitate the picture becoming a reality?
- If single, what preparations have you made in your life to be a man who is ready for marriage? What is your financial status? Have you prepared yourself for a family?
- What do you have to offer a woman? What does the woman in your life have to offer to you?
- How selfish are you? How selfless? What things do you need to surrender?
- Are you willing to have a godly courtship? a godly marriage? Do you feel responsible for maintaining this standard in your relationship?

For Her

"An unmarried woman or virgin is concerned about the Lord's affairs: Her aim is to be devoted to the Lord in both body and spirit. But a married woman is concerned about the affairs of this world—how she can please her husband" (1 Corinthians 7:34). "A wife of noble character who can find? She is worth far more than rubies" (Proverb 31:10). A woman must recognize her value but also be able to shift her priorities to focus on the man in her life. Then she can effectively add value to his life and to her household.

- Do you have a plan for your life?
- If single, what are you doing to prepare yourself for marriage? Do you have criteria for the man you want in your life? What character traits, personality, and qualities do you desire?
- What skills are you cultivating for creating a secure household?
- What does the picture of your family life look like as you envision it? Is it a realistic picture? Where do you need to readjust the picture?
- How selfish are you? How selfless? Which areas do you need to work on?
- What do you have to offer the man in your life? Are these things apparent to him? Does he celebrate these things about you?

For You Both

As both partners remain cognizant of the value of the other, it will free you to celebrate and encourage each other. A little bit of praise does wonders for increasing your passion and love for each other.

- In what ways can you continue to cultivate your friendship and love for each other?
- How can you maintain a standard of godliness in your courtship? in your marriage?
- Are you clear on your roles in the relationship? How can you maintain a healthy balance? Are you able to be flexible according to each other's needs?
- How honest are you about your needs and desires with each other? How can you nurture deeper communication?
- What plans do you have for the future? Where do you agree? Disagree? How can you find common ground?

9

WHAT A LITTLE MOONLIGHT WILL DO

Romancing Your Beloved

I have loved you with an everlasting love;
I have drawn you with loving-kindness.

JEREMIAH 31:3

The Proverbs 31 man knows how to romance his woman.

My former pastor's wife, Sister Juanita Smith, once said to me, "Michelle, make sure that when you marry, you say yes to the man that you like, love, and are in love with. If one of those three is missing, don't do it!" Back in that day, I overspiritualized everything until it made no earthly sense. Sister Smith knew that I lacked the ability to balance my spirituality with practical understanding and application. Her advice saved me from making some major mistakes in the love arena. I think these are sound words for everyone. Sister Smith's rationale is very simple: In any relationship, love ebbs and flows. On days when you don't have goose bumps, your love for your mate will motivate you to continue the give-and-take. On days when you don't feel so loving, the fact that you like your mate and generally enjoy his or her company will sustain you until waves of refreshment cause your love level to rise again.

When it comes to romance, without a doubt, it's the little things that light the fire of a woman's heart or douse the flame. Unless schooled in the details of romance, men often find themselves at a loss when their wife does not respond to their attention. In today's "go go go, rush rush rush" culture, the attention paid to romance in days gone by has waned. Even so, women still harbor secret wishes for real romance. They long for a relationship with a man who knows how to make them feel special and who will court them both before and after marriage.

WHEN LOVE IS IN BLOOM

As when nurturing a delicate flower, time and care are required for cultivating love and passion in a relationship because men and women have such diverging needs. Women are moved by what they hear, while men are moved by what they see. Men seem to have no problem leaping into a romantic mood. I like to make the comparison between microwaves and Crockpots when thinking of men's and women's romantic styles. Men are like microwaves: They can heat up fast and cool off even faster. Women are like Crockpots: It takes them a while to heat up, but when they're hot, they're hot!

Men and women—more specifically, you and your spouse—need

to learn each other's love language, take the cues, and adjust the courting moves. Every man and woman has very different romantic needs. What works with Sally won't work with Sue. It is good not to leave this area to assumption. Ask your partner questions, lots of questions, about what makes him or her feel loved. No one has ESP, so it's not worth pretending that you do.

Many couples are guilty of being romantic throughout the courtship and then letting that element of their relationship languish after wedding vows have been exchanged. Marriage is not the time to get lazy! As a matter of fact, I would dare to say this is when the real romance should begin, now that you have permission to fulfill its promise.

Timeless, classical music generally follows a recognizable pattern: There is the introduction, which usually starts off rather subdued. As more and more instrumentation is added, the music builds and swells to a crescendo. The rhythm may even quicken to give the piece more drama and urgency. The music builds to the point of exploding, and then it ebbs away, leaving only the emotions one experienced while listening to it. Such is the dance of love between a couple.

> *Romance is biblical. God is a shameless lover. He is not inhibited when it comes to expressing His love.*

THE ROMANTIC HEART

Tenderness and sensitivity are words that scare most men, perhaps because they fear someone will question their masculinity. Yet God, Creator of men, embodies these traits and exhibits them in pursuit of His wife, the corporate church. Constantly wooing her to His side, He speaks words of endearment: I will never leave you or forsake you. My thoughts toward you outnumber the grains of sand on the earth (see Hebrews 13:5; Psalm 139:17-18). His conversation to His bride is laden with potent promises of His faithfulness and the blessings He has in store for her: Oh taste and see that I am good. I will supply all your needs. My goodness and mercy will follow you forever. At my right hand are pleasures evermore (see Psalm 34:8; Philippians 4:19; Psalm 23:6; 16:11).

God cares for His bride by washing her, dressing her in rich garments, watching over her at all times, letting her know that He is thinking of her constantly, and meeting all of her needs. He continually thinks of ways to draw her closer to Him. When she wanders away from His side, He calls her back to Himself and reveals more of His heart to her. Romance is biblical. God is a shameless lover. He is not inhibited when it comes to expressing His love.

Solomon, king of Israel, should probably be considered the king of romance. That man could rap—no wonder the Shulamite woman was sick with love! I don't know a woman alive who would not be madly in love with a man who treated her the way Solomon treated the Shulamite.

First, he shows up in such a spectacular way—on chariots!—that everyone is impressed with his show of love. Every woman can tell you the movie scenes that caused her to swoon in her chair—scenes like the one in *An Officer and a Gentleman* where our hero Richard Gere marches through the factory and sweeps Debra Winger off her feet in the presence of all her coworkers. Movies boast scene after scene of men publicly letting the world know of their love for the woman in their lives. Many women fill movie theaters to vicariously live through the lives of the women on the screen whose dashing men dare to try to win their love. Realistically speaking, not many men are going to march into a woman's workplace or show up in a limousine or climb a fire escape to sweep their fair maiden away. Still, the underlying desire is clear and can be accomplished in a man's own individual way. A woman longs to be possessed by a man not as an acquisition but as a treasure. When a man makes a woman and everyone around her know that she is his pearl of great price, she feels loved.

The next thing Solomon does is praise her beauty, in spite of the Shulamite's own insecurities in this area. He praises her and speaks of all her attributes that he admires. He notices things about her that no one else has noticed and remarks on it. Every woman wants to know her man finds her beautiful. She seeks affirmation from him. Many men who were not raised in homes where praise and affirmation were given freely might not be vocal in this area. Give it a try! Women spend a lot of time and money in order to be attractive to members of the opposite sex. Though some would say they enjoy looking good for themselves, the bonus for most is when a man notices and compliments them. When a man makes a woman feel beautiful, his praise frees her from her inhibitions and releases her to love him.

Next, Solomon adorns the beauty he celebrates. He offers his lover gifts of jewelry and pledges his love to her. He tells her at one point that she is a "lily among thorns" in comparison to other women. Well! What woman doesn't want to know that her man only has eyes for her? What woman doesn't like presents, whether they be jewelry, flowers, a wonderful card, or something personally creative? Presents are big to a woman because it says to her that she was in the thoughts of the man that she loves even while they were apart. Not only did he think of her, he went to the extra effort to prove it with physical evidence.

THE PURSUIT OF PASSION

Solomon pursued his woman with genuine honesty. He was himself, not trying to be cool or slick, and she loved every minute of it. He openly admitted that she had ravished his heart; he was overcome by one glance from her. He became vulnerable to her, and she in turn melted in his arms. Every woman wants a man who will share his heart and feelings with her. Playing "he loves me, he loves me not" only breeds an insecurity in her that will stop the flow of love between them. Because Solomon pursued his love relentlessly, she was able to articulate why she loved him. When her friends asked her why her lover was better than any other, she was quick to list all of his wonderful virtues. By the time she was finished talking about how great he was, all of her friends were ready to help her find him! (See Song of Songs 5:9–6:1.) A Proverbs 31 man leaves a lasting impression on his woman's mind that causes her thoughts to be filled with him.

In marriage, a couple establishes routines to keep their house and home in order. But love should never become routine. The man as well as the woman must become inventive when it comes to keeping the spirit of romance alive.

Solomon told his love that she was a secret garden of delights. Check out the dialogue between these two: "You are a garden locked

Good lovers are not selfish lovers. They seek ways to please their beloved.

up, my sister, my bride; you are a spring enclosed, a sealed fountain. Your plants are an orchard of pomegranates with choice fruits, with henna and nard, nard and saffron, calamus and cinnamon, with every kind of incense tree, with myrrh and aloes and all the finest spices. You are a garden fountain, a well of flowing water streaming down from Lebanon.

Awake, north wind, and come, south wind! Blow on my garden, that its fragrance may spread abroad. Let my lover come into his garden and taste its choice fruits" (Song of Songs 4:12-16). All of the spices he mentioned were costly spices used for healing and anointing the body. Their fragrance was exotic and haunting. In other words, he was trying to let her know how her love affected him. Her love fed him, healed him, and left something on his mind. Every woman needs to know that what she has to offer her man is appreciated and enjoyed.

Good lovers are not selfish lovers. They seek ways to please their beloved. Frank communication, which might have to be learned, is central in making this occur. Take a deep breath and dive in! A woman risks exposure by sharing her needs, but each of you will feel safer if the risk is mutual. A man who takes the time to find out what pleases his wife and takes the time to satisfy her will be rewarded: A satisfied woman seeks to satisfy her man.

As his secret garden, she cultivates a wonderful array of things that will make her an oasis for her man. The Proverbs 31 woman covered her bed, making their bedroom a sanctuary—a place where love could be cultivated. The bedroom is a sacred place for secrets that do not leave the room. It should be the place where both feel free to be vulnerable and transparent—naked and unashamed.

In order to be naked and unashamed, no one can bring extra baggage to the room. Faithfulness and honor are foundational for two people to be unreserved in their passion for each other. No one else should be a distracting factor in your union. If you have appetizers before the main entrée, one is seldom able to fully enjoy or consume the entire entrée. One of the qualities God has placed in a woman is intuition. Even if she doesn't have proof, she will know when she is dealing with a man with a divided heart.

In several places in Scripture, God encourages men to put their all into loving their wives. He wants them to enjoy loving their wives. He compares the love of a wife to a source of refreshing:

Drink water from your own cistern, running water from your own well. Should your springs overflow in the streets, your streams of water in the public squares? Let them be yours alone, never to be shared with strangers. May your fountain be blessed, and may you rejoice in the wife of your youth. A loving doe, a graceful deer—may her breasts satisfy you always, may you ever be captivated by her love. Why be captivated, my son, by an adulteress? Why embrace the bosom of another man's wife? For a man's ways are in full view of the LORD, and he examines all his paths. (Proverbs 5:15-21)

An ample composite of renderings from several different translations of this scripture read like this: "Drink water from your own cistern and running water from your own spring; do not let your well overflow into the road, your runnels of water pour into the street; let them be yours alone, not shared with strangers" (NEB). "Let your fountain [of human life] be blessed...and rejoice in the wife of your youth" (AMP). "Loving as the hind, and affectionate as the gazelle, let her bosom ever satisfy thee; and with her love be thou ever transported" (SPRL). "Let her affection fill you at all times with delight, be infatuated always with her love" (RSV). "Let her breasts intoxicate you always, with her love be continually ravished" (SAG). "Let her breasts give you rapture, let her love ever ravish you" (MOF). "Hers the breasts that ever fill you with delight, hers the love that ever holds you captive" (JB). "Be it her bosom that steals away thy senses with the delight of a lover who loves still" (KNOX).

There are two points here that beg not to be overlooked. First, the overall context of what all these translations suggest is that you should enjoy intimacies with your wife as a lover who loves continuously through marriage. A husband and wife must consciously return to the first feelings they had for each other. Forgive each other for any offenses that have gotten in the way, and then go back and restore the passion you had for each other early in your marriage. Whatever needs to be done to stir up love in the relationship should be done so that lovemaking is not an act, but a response to the love that flows between the two of you. There will be times in a marriage when one partner or the other will sacrifice his or her fatigue or distractions (job stress, children, and so on) and make love for no other reason than to meet a spouse's physical need. This is when the response to love is a conscious act that God will honor by surprising you with pleasure in the midst of your effort.

The next point is deep, so pay attention: Even if "the other woman" is a single woman, she is someone else's wife, already foreordained to meet the husband at God's appointed time; therefore, she should not be compromised. Adultery is the quickest killer of love there is. God Himself says that He will make life hard for the adulterous man. He spoke through the prophet Malachi saying, "The LORD is acting as the witness between you and the wife of your youth, because you have broken faith with her, though she is your partner, the wife of your marriage covenant. Has not the Lord made them one? In flesh and spirit they are his. And why one? Because he was seeking godly offspring. So guard yourself in your spirit, and do not break faith with the wife of your youth" (Malachi 2:14-15). Keep your love pure and your passion high by being faithful. Your integrity will give your woman the confidence she needs to love without reserve.

Women, be mindful that men also need to know that their attentions are enjoyed. The man who wonders about himself as a man is exposed to seeking validation from the wrong sources if his wife will not supply the affirmation he needs. David, king of Israel, was quick to point this out to his wife Michal when she criticized him for dancing in the streets. The Bible says she remained childless for the rest of her days (see 2 Samuel 6:20-23). Who can say whether her barrenness was from God's judgment or David's neglect of her from that moment on? The bottom line is this: Don't give your mate the motivation to seek affection elsewhere.

Don't be naive because you are a Christian. The divorce rate continues to rise in the church even as it seems to level out in the secular arena. This may be because an increasing number of couples "in the world" are delaying marriage or deciding not to marry at all.

PICTURE-PERFECT LOVE

The love between a man and a woman is supposed to be symbolic of the love between Christ and the church. Therefore, we can consider sex the natural parallel to the spiritual act of worship. What is sex? What is worship? They are both the act of giving all that you have and all that you are to the one whom you love. Each involves bestowing all your love, honor, and praise on that loved one, whether it be Christ or a mate. In another parallel of worship, consider the analogy I made in chapter 9: The woman is like the Holy of Holies, and the man is like the high priest. As the priest brings an offering into the Holy of Holies and ministers there, the praises go up, the glory of God comes down, and we experience a foretaste of the immense pleasure we will experience when we become one with Christ forever more.

A foretaste of heaven, this is what God meant for a husband and wife to experience in this sacred and special time together. Sex is sacred to God and must not be perverted or polluted by premature intimacy or inordinate acts. Yet the world has reduced sex to a performance-oriented activity of no lasting significance. Intimacy between a husband and wife was not designed to be an "act," but a yielding and a response to each other's love. Believers must get the world out of their bedrooms and return to the garden—

> When a real man of integrity knows that his partner has entrusted her heart to him, the knowledge breeds careful responsibility in his own life. He will not want to disappoint his beloved.

return to God's first intention for a man and a woman to "know" each other on a level that transcends the flesh. This is the beauty and mystery of oneness that God ordained for man and woman. The ultimate act of servanthood is to give all you have for the benefit of the other. This sacrifice binds a couple together in an intimate embrace of "knowing." Here they conceive of a deeper love than they have ever imagined, and it manifests itself in the fruit of their commitment to each other.

In most scriptures that discuss the sexual union, the phrase *to know* is used for this term. "And Adam knew Eve his wife, and she conceived" (Genesis 4:1, RSV). This word *knowing* actually meant that they made love. But the word *knowing* is more accurate. Perhaps this is why we shouldn't "know" everybody! A husband and wife should "know" things about each other that no one else knows: hidden mysteries, so to speak. When we know God, we also conceive. We conceive of the fruit of the Spirit and bear the attributes of Christ to the world. When a man and a woman "know" each other, they conceive the fruit of the love that they bear to each other, whether it be in the form of children or a deeper bond of love. No encounter should be fruitless.

Understanding God's design for sex allows a couple to come together, understanding fully that their connection to each other is far greater than just the physical.

SETTING THE MOOD

The mood for love is set far before entering the bedroom. A man's loving ways and attention set the atmosphere for the woman to respond in love to him and vice versa. Romance must be nurtured. Much of romance starts in the mind, beginning with the not-so-obvious things such as a loving expression, a tantalizing word, a gentle touch. A man should appeal to a woman's mind as well as her body. As woman must in turn appeal to a man's mind and senses.

When questioning couples who are struggling to enjoy intimacy, as I mentioned before, I have found that in most cases where the woman does not desire the man, she has been wounded in some way by him. She has been harboring secret anger or an unresolved issue between them. Just as a man might not be in the mood for intimacy when he is worried over business or financial matters, or when he doubts his manhood in areas where he has placed high expectations on himself, women struggle with their desirability and interest in intimacy when they feel they have been ignored, misunderstood, betrayed, or criticized.

The man thinks she's just cold, but she is cold for a reason. It has nothing to do with her body but everything to do with her mind and her spirit. A husband must be sensitive to his wife's needs on every level, not just the physical. When sensitive to her emotions, he can do a better job of making sure that disagreements are resolved and that the lines of communication are clear on any issue that might be a problem between them.

As God calls His bride to Himself saying, "Come now, let us reason together.... Though your sins are like scarlet, they shall be white as snow" (Isaiah 1:18), a husband must be willing to wash away offense, to call his wife to him in all willingness to reason together with her to resolve issues that block their ability to express the love between them. Though this is much easier said than done, it is an act of the will. The decision to pursue reconciliation must be in place. A made-up mind has everything to do with doing the work it takes to maintain a healthy love relationship. At the bottom line, both partners need to settle in their own minds that divorce is not an option, and so elbow grease will be required to keep a clean slate between them.

Keeping in mind that sexual intimacy is only one aspect in the scheme of romance, establish other love rituals between you. As a teenager I recall an incident at my house that I will never forget. My dad had pulled all the way out of the driveway to go to work. My mother and I were washing dishes in the kitchen when we noticed he had pulled back into driveway and was heading toward the house. My mother asked him what he had forgotten, and he replied, "I forgot my kiss." He tenderly kissed her good-bye and headed back to work. My mother giggled for the rest of the day. At the time I thought, *How silly was that?* Today, this is still the rule: No one leaves the house without a good-bye kiss. My father does not sleep well until my mother is back home by his side. She is confident of his love for her in part because of the little things he does to constantly reinforce their connection to each other.

No one will ever be able to explain why a call from a spouse in the middle of the day means so much. Why a tender look can cause one to thrill inside. Why a lingering touch can haunt someone all day. But this is the subtle dance of romance.

Motivated by Love and Service

In our relationship with God, He does not rely on our fear of Him to prompt our obedience. He banks on our love for Him being the motivating force. As we reflect on His goodness toward us, our hearts should be filled with grateful and loving obedience. His patience toward us should make us not want to test it. The blessings He gives should make us want to give back even more. His protectiveness should incite a desire to honor His Spirit that is living within us. When the lover is loving as he should, the beloved wants to be her best for him.

In such a scenario, love, not duty, becomes the motivation for every response. Dutiful love becomes an empty act at best, but uninhibited love flows from the passion that has been inspired in the heart of an individual who feels completely loved. The Proverbs 31 man knows that when the heart of his woman securely rests in the fact that she is loved, she can face her world joyfully. She will guard his home and his secrets with faithful adoration and give herself to him with joyful abandon.

A related ingredient in a healthy romance is that of serving the one you love. Sometimes we are so caught up in the traditional teaching most receive on submission that another text is seriously overlooked: "Submit to one another out of reverence for Christ" (Ephesians 5:21). Just as Jesus washed His disciples' feet, even though He was greater than they, a man is called to serve the woman in his life. A glowing newlywed wife told me: "Every morning he wakes me up with a kiss and coffee before he leaves for work. It makes me feel so special! And then he will leave me a little note with something sweet for me to read before I start my day. It has caused me to love him even more than before."

Sometimes romance can be as simple as being thoughtful and helpful. A couple has to be able to discern the rigors of their schedule and how to balance the chores between them. Though some tasks are traditionally expected of women, a woman is much more willing to be the wife that is expected when she feels she has assistance from her mate.

A man returns home weary from work. So does a woman. Even as a stay-at-home mom, the demands are great. Both partners must be sensitive to the needs of the other. They must serve each other all the while listening and helping each other. They must take up the slack and work to make life easier for each other. No one is in the mood for love if they are exhausted. Share the load. Balance the yoke between you. Be there for your mate, and he or she will be there for you, to meet not only your needs but your desires as well.

In times of weariness, remember that sex with your partner should be considered a ministry. As you bless your partner, you in turn will get blessed. Ever thought about going to exercise but just didn't feel like it? Chances are once you made yourself get started, you got into it and ended up feeling better for it in the end. That's how it works. The body needs to expend energy in order to regenerate it. Don't simply rely on your feelings; your will must be involved. We don't always feel like serving the Lord, yet we know it is best to do so; therefore, we will to be obedient. In the end we are blessed, and He honors our submission to His Word.

In the same way, marriage partners must learn to give and take on those days when they don't feel like responding. "The husband should fulfill his marital duty to his wife, and likewise the wife to her husband. The wife's body does not belong to her alone but also to her husband. In the same way, the husband's body does not belong to him alone but also to his wife. Do not deprive each other except by mutual consent and for a time, so that you may devote yourselves to prayer. Then come together again so that Satan will not tempt you because of your lack of self-control" (1 Corinthians 7:3-5). Just as we are called to present our bodies as a living sacrifice to God, which is our reasonable act of worship, it is a reasonable act of service to your mate.

Women who struggle with enjoying sexual intimacy must take the time to allow God to heal their hearts and minds, especially if this response is borne out of past experiences that have been painful. Seek counseling and ask God to heal your memories if you have been violated. Some women were raised to regard sex as a dirty and unpleasant chore, yet God Himself created it to be a beautiful exchange between the lover and the beloved. If physical pain is involved, consult your doctor. Don't allow yourself to be robbed of the pleasure that God wants you to experience with your mate. Men, don't take these issues to heart as personal rejection, but show sensitivity in this area. Partner with your wife in getting the help she needs. Serve her and she will love you for it.

In the mood for love? Clear the way for leaving your cares behind as you lose yourselves in each other's arms.

Let him kiss me with the kisses of his mouth—
for your love is better than wine.

SONG OF SONGS 1:2

The Proverbs 31 man views the love he shares with his wife as a sacred gift to give and receive.

FOR REFLECTION AND DISCUSSION

For Him

"Let love and faithfulness never leave you; bind them around your neck, write them on the tablet of your heart" (Proverbs 3:3). "Enjoy life with your wife, whom you love" (Ecclesiastes 9:9). "He has taken me to the banquet hall, and his banner over me is love. Strengthen me with raisins, refresh me with apples, for I am faint with love" (Song of Songs 2:4-5). "How delightful is your love, my sister, my bride! How much more pleasing is your love than wine, and the fragrance of your perfume than any spice!" (Song of Songs 4:10). A man must keep in mind that romance is a constant in marriage, not a momentary pleasure.

- Do you have a romantic nature? What are some romantic things that you can do to charge the atmosphere between you and your wife with love?
- What is your attitude toward sexual intimacy? Is it an expression of love to you or is it a source of release? How do you seek to please her first in your intimate moments?
- What do you need from her to help you make your time together more pleasurable?
- Are you faithful to your wife? What things do you do to make her feel secure? beautiful? loved?
- What special surprise can you plan to spark her romantic mood?

For Her

"I slept but my heart was awake. Listen! My lover is knocking: 'Open to me, my sister, my darling, my dove, my flawless one. My head is drenched with dew, my hair with the dampness of the night'" (Song of Songs 5:2). "How beautiful you are and how pleasing, O love, with your delights!" (Song of Songs 7:6). "Let us go early to the vineyards to see if the vines have budded, if their blossoms have opened, and if the pomegranates are in bloom—there I will give you my love" (Song of Songs 7:12). A woman must be sensitive to the needs of her husband, regarding her love as a precious gift to be given as well as a profound ministry to his spirit.

- What is your attitude toward sexual intimacy? Is it something you enjoy? Is it something you dread? If yes, why? How can you partner with your husband and God to gain healing?
- What other things stop you from being open to intimacy?
- What do you need from your husband to make you more desirous of intimacy with him?
- What can he do to make you feel loved? Have you discussed these things with him?
- How do you feel about your body? yourself? What do you need to do to feel more comfortable in sharing yourself with your mate?

For You Both

As both partners take the time to nurture each other's need for romance, the seeds of love will burrow deeper into the soil of each one's heart. The seeds will then sprout and bloom and produce sweeter fruit to feed each other as well as others in their circle of love.

- What is your mate's response to you in romantic moments? Do you discuss your intimate needs and desires with each other?
- What are some of the things that you did in courtship that you no longer do? Why? Are you willing to return to your first love?

- What are the things that kill your passion? What ignites it?
- What types of things can you do to set the atmosphere for romance in your home?
- How can you go about making sure that you set aside time just for each other? What do you need from your mate in order to feel loved and desired?

10

THE ULTIMATE MODEL
OF MANHOOD

Following Your Perfect Example

"In that day," declares the LORD, "you will call me 'my husband';
you will no longer call me 'my master.'"

HOSEA 2:16

The Proverbs 31 husband embodies the nature of Christ.

By now everyone is probably thinking, *Who can live up to all of this stuff? There is no man on the face of the earth who can be all of the things we've talked about. This is a fruitless exercise...* Allow me to encourage you. "Jesus replied, 'What is impossible with men is possible with God'" (Luke 18:27). There is only one thing that is impossible for God to do, and that is to lie. If God is made strong in our weakness, then it stands to reason that when the Spirit of Christ dwells in a man or a woman, he or she possesses the same qualities, attributes, and character traits of Jesus Himself! With this in mind, every man has the potential to be a Proverbs 31 man if he allows Christ to reign and rule in his life.

Truly Jesus is the ultimate model of the Proverbs 31 male. He is the Ultimate Bridegroom. He is the prototype of the knight in shining armor that every woman dreams of, with one difference: He is King of kings and Lord of lords, though He is also the Prince of Peace. Loving Him brings peace to the hearts of all who know Him. He is the totality of the reconciliation we seek with God, ourselves, and with all of humankind.

How is this possible? Because Jesus is the expression of God's love for us. We, as adopted members of God's household, are called to be the same, expressing love not from a human perspective but from God's. As we allow Him to control our nature, we are transformed to reflect His image in our relationships with others. Love is no longer about how we feel or what we get from another. It becomes about what we can give and express to those around us.

THE CONSISTENCY OF LOVE

It is unfortunate that in too many homes a spouse is not the recipient of the love and care that others outside the home receive from his or her mate. Such mates know how to put on the "church face." They're saints at church and abroad, but you wouldn't know it once they get home. Yet we are asked in the book of James: "My brothers, can a fig tree bear olives, or a grapevine bear figs? Neither can a salt spring produce fresh water" (3:12). As Christians, we are called to walk consistently. Jesus was consistent. He treated everyone with the same love, rich or poor, intelligent or not. He was a conduit of God's love to the world.

What is love? We love to rattle off 1 Corinthians 13 without really internalizing the text:

> Love is patient, love is kind. It does not envy, it does not boast, it is not proud. It is not rude, it is not self-seeking, it is not easily angered, it keeps no record of wrongs. Love does not delight in evil but rejoices with the truth. It always protects, always trusts, always hopes, always perseveres.
>
> Love never fails. But where there are prophecies, they will cease; where there are tongues, they will be stilled; where there is knowledge, it will pass away. For we know in part and we prophesy in part, but when perfection comes, the imperfect disappears. When I was a child, I talked like a child, I thought like a child, I reasoned like a child. When I became a man, I put childish ways behind me. Now we see but a poor reflection as in a mirror; then we shall see face to face. Now I know in part; then I shall know fully, even as I am fully known.
>
> And now these three remain: faith, hope and love. But the greatest of these is love.
>
> Follow the way of love. (13:4–14:1)

In the passage before this one, Paul wrote that if you possess all the greatest spiritual gifts, including faith, but do not have love, you are in essence pretty worthless. Love puts a spin on everything you do. Without it, your behaviors are merely self-consumed prideful acts borne out of ungodly intentions. The man who goes through the motions of taking care of business, paying the household bills, and looking good to the world but doesn't love his wife and children is not a hero in God's eyes or the eyes of his family. Love makes the difference. Many a poor family that has little more than one another has a joy that surpasses that of wealthy families. When love is all you have, it tends to be distributed more freely.

THE WAY OF LOVE

But let's consider the text above from 1 Corinthians 13. Let's break it down into layman's terms. We all are well aware of what people do that makes us feel unloved. But what can we be cognizant of in our own exchanges with others? For one, true love is slow to lose patience. It looks for a way of being constructive. God looked down from heaven and saw our faults and found a constructive way to solve the problem between Him and man by sacrificing His Son's life for our sakes. In the same way, we must learn to make sacrifices for one another.

Jesus is slow to anger and patient with us, His bride, the church. Paul reminded us that nothing can separate us from the love of God (see Romans 8:39). In spite of us, God extends His grace and mercy to love us unconditionally, even as Christ hung on the cross! Looking at those who cried, "Crucify Him!" He prayed for them: "Father, forgive them, for they do not know what they are doing" (Luke 23:34). And that was the truth. They didn't know what they were doing, or they would not have done it.

> When a man and a woman "know" each other, they conceive the fruit of the love that they bear to each other, whether it be in the form of children or a deeper love. No encounter should be fruitless.

Isn't it interesting how we choose whom we are willing to be patient with? Usually, we are most patient with those we believe don't know any better—babies, cats, dogs—and that might be about it. When it comes to grown folks, we typically lose it at the first offense! Most of the time, I have come to learn, a person's offensive act is not about you at all. The offense is some culmination of a lot of unknown factors. Instead of reacting to an offensive person in kind, extend to him or her loving patience and seek a constructive way to deal with the matter at hand. This course of action can free that person.

Love is not anxious to impress and knows no jealousy. Jesus, though He was Lord of lords, did not flaunt His greatness while on earth. He readily admitted He had no place to lay His head! All He really offered to those around Him was Himself, and that is all He required from those who chose to follow Him. Despite their lack of understanding, and no matter how often they did all the wrong things, He loved them with an everlasting love, exercising patience and painstakingly teaching them truths that would give them life.

When you truly love someone, there is no need for that person to win your love with showmanship. Love loves simply because a person is who he is. Love loves in spite of what she has or has not accomplished. Love loves heart to heart, spirit to spirit. It delights in the inner qualities of the beloved. It covers that person's failings. "Love covers over all wrongs" (Proverbs 10:12).

True love is not jealous because it completely trusts the beloved! It always believes the best concerning that person. Jesus released people to be all who they were. He did not force anyone to love Him. He wanted their love to be freely given. The Spirit of God guards us jealously (see 2 Corinthians 11:2), but not with the earthly possessiveness that we know. His jealousy is rooted in a protective longing to keep us out of harm's way. He longs to keep us from becoming entangled with those people, things, and situations that He knows are not good for us. He does not demand that we become unwilling robots, serving Him out of duty. He invites us to taste and see that He is good (see Psalm 34:8), then He entrusts us with the choice to worship Him.

God releases us by giving us the precious gift of choice. This is the example that we must follow in our earthly relationships. Mistrust in our mate breeds a reason for mistrust and begins a vicious cycle of deceit. But when a real man of integrity knows that his partner has entrusted her heart to him, the knowledge breeds careful responsibility in his own life. He will not want to disappoint his beloved. The same is true of women.

It is true that many people have entrusted their heart to the wrong person far too soon, which leads only to disappointment and heartbreak. By the time someone trustworthy enters their life, the trustworthy person will have double the work to do to earn the other's confidence. Sometimes the task is impossible, leading to further loss for the person who was wounded in the first place. In these instances, the enemy can cause the one in pain to believe that all members of the opposite sex do little more than inflict pain. To cling to this belief is to forfeit future chances at true love. Those who know Christ must cling to the hope that is stronger than doubt.

Love is not rude or selfish. It doesn't insist on its own rights. It is not self-seeking and does not insist on having its own way. It is always considerate, looking out for the interest of the beloved, even if doing so means personal loss. A loving person can do this knowing that what will be reaped in the long run is far greater than what was sacrificed. Jesus gave up all His heavenly rights when He chose to leave heaven and come to earth on our behalf. He had the right to be respected and worshiped, yet He surrendered all of that to be lied to, abused, and crucified. But oh, what He gained on that resurrection day! He gained the world for Himself! All because He

How many of us have been personally relieved by His graciousness and yet are slow to extend that same graciousness to others?

was willing to surrender the privileges of His station and humble Himself to gain the greater good.

Your attitude should be the same as that of Christ Jesus:

> Who, being in very nature God,
>   did not consider equality with God something to be grasped,
> but made himself nothing,
>   taking the very nature of a servant,
>   being made in human likeness.
> And being found in appearance as a man,
>   he humbled himself
>   and became obedient to death—even death on a cross!
> Therefore God exalted him to the highest place
>   and gave him the name that is above every name,
> that at the name of Jesus every knee should bow,
>   in heaven and on earth and under the earth,
> and every tongue confess that Jesus Christ is Lord,
>   to the glory of God the Father. (Philippians 2:5-11)

When we became Christians, our rights became hidden in Christ. Similarly, when a man and woman come together, they cannot cling to their personal rights. They are one and must give and take. Their "rights" are now collective. Both must be willing to sacrifice personal treasures and desires for the greater good of the relationship.

Love is not quick to take offense; it doesn't keep a scorecard of wrongs. Oh my, if Jesus wrote down every little thing we do, we would all be in trouble! Yet He does exactly the opposite when we confess our sin to Him. He flings them "as far as the east is from the west, so far has he removed our transgressions from us" (Psalm 103:12). Again having compassion on us, He treads our sins underfoot and hurls all of our iniquities into the depths of the sea (see Micah 7:19). He releases us from the debt of sin by covering us with His love, mercy, and forgiveness. Jesus even released and forgave those who deliberately hurt Him. He did not charge the offenses to their account; instead, He asked God to erase the marks against them by taking their sins upon Himself once and for all.

In the day-to-day details of life, a husband and wife must make a conscious effort to minimize being touchy or irritable. Love does not jump to conclusions and assume the other person is trying to deliberately hurt them. This is why communication is key. Let your partner know what hurts you. Your spouse may be unaware of how you are really feeling. In most cases, offenses are rooted in transferred pain or ignorance. Though your loved one might offend you again and again, embrace the grace of God. Don't we continually offend God in the same areas until He completes His work in us? We are all works in progress, hindered by our own humanity, but in grace we grow into perfect love. The person who loves seeks to find a remedy for the root cause of the offense and not for the surface action. He or she seeks to heal rather than inflict further injury.

Love is never glad when others go wrong but is always glad when truth prevails. It can overlook faults. Love is always slow to expose and always eager to believe the best of the person. Though Jesus sees us as we truly are, He does not broadcast our sin to hurt us. When He looks at us sitting in the middle of our messes, He does not proudly say, "I told you so!" He does not find joy in our pain or in the consequences we bring on ourselves. Instead, He grieves because, when we hurt, He hurts. He doesn't rub our faces in our mistakes. Instead, He lovingly picks up the pieces of our shattered spirit and mends it. How many of us have been personally relieved by His graciousness and yet are slow to extend that same graciousness to others?

Wives, your husband might always leave his socks in the middle of the floor and leave the toilet seat up at night. He may do something even bigger that constantly upsets you. Cover it with grace. Pick up the socks, lower the seat, and whisper a prayer. It takes less energy to right the oversight than to fuss about it. Men, your wife might always point out everything you're doing wrong. Maybe she fusses endlessly about things that you find trivial. Cover it with grace. Stop and say, "I hear you and I'll try to do better next time."

This man Jesus, who embodies all that we have discussed, sets an example for men to aspire to. He is the epitome of what women can lovingly require—not by demand but by inspiration and nurturing—of the men in their lives.

Then apply yourself to doing just that while anticipating the reward of her smile. Look beyond the daily idiosyncrasies of the person you love. Discover and celebrate his or her greater goodness. Perhaps you will see that even the things that irritate you are part of his or her love language to you. Don't let the little irritations stress you. Instead, allow them to stretch your love beyond its present boundaries.

Perfect love knows no limit to its endurance. It hopes under all circumstances. Love gives us the power to endure anything, including the loss of finances and good health, personal crises, the betrayal of love, or a wayward child. If a man and woman choose to cling to love when weathering the storms of life, they can make it back to the harbors of restoration. Spiritual gifts will fade and so will natural ones. Only love will endure.

GROWING UP

Love can endure, however, only if we choose to mature. We all head into a relationship with a rosy view of what love should look and feel like, but then the real work sets in. The work of exercising patience, of forgiving and forgiving again, of overlooking offenses real or imagined. Our example of love, Jesus, does exactly these things with us. Yes, as we walk this road of love laden with wonderful and terrible surprises, we are all still learning. Yet no one can deny that it is an exciting journey! If we never complete the trip, we will never reach the reward. Perhaps that's why Paul ended his sermon on love by saying, "Follow the way of love" (1 Corinthians 14:1). A compilation of this key phrase from other translations might read, "Keep on pursuing love, hotly pursue it, make it your aim, make it your great quest, seek it earnestly." Just as Jesus constantly woos and pursues us, we are asked to do the same with our brothers and sisters in Christ—especially those to whom we have committed our lives.

This man Jesus, who embodies all that we have discussed, sets an example for men to aspire to. He is the epitome of what women can lovingly require—not by demand but by inspiration and nurturing—of the men in their lives.

Here He is, sitting in the heavenlies, surrounded and worshiped by an adoring heavenly host fully aware of His glory, power, and might. But one day from the windows of heaven He leans forward on His throne and sees a woman that He must have, the church. In spite of all that it will cost Him to leave heaven, He volunteers for this rescue mission. "I must have her," He says to Himself. Stepping down out of glory, He clothes himself in earthly form, but not as a full-grown man. No, he starts from scratch. He wants to relate to all of her experiences, weaknesses, temptations, and trials. He chooses to be born of a woman and to grow up, to endure the process of maturing, to learn obedience through suffering, and to get firsthand knowledge of this woman's emotions and inner struggles. He pursues her even when she won't listen to Him. In the face of her blatant rejection, still He chooses to fight the dragon, Satan, to win her hand, and to die. He surrenders all that He is in order to win her to Himself.

When He knows the end is near, He is not deterred. He does not decide that she is not worth the price that He must pay—separation from the Father. (Even Jesus had to leave the Father and cleave to His wife, by taking on her sin to make her one with Him!) He simply bows His head in prayer to His Father and says,

> Holy Father, keep them in your own care—all those you have
> given me.... I guarded them so that not one perished.... I have
> told them many things...so that they would be filled with my
> joy.... Make them pure and holy through teaching them your
> words of truth. As you sent me into the world, I am sending them
> into the world, and I consecrate myself to meet their need for
> growth in truth and holiness.... My prayer for all of them is that
> they will be of one heart and mind, just as you and I are, Father—
> that just as you are in me and I am in you, so they will be in us....
> Father, I want them with me—these you've given me—so that
> they can see my glory.... I have revealed you to them and will
> keep on revealing you so that the mighty love you have for me
> may be in them, and I in them. (John 17:11-26, TLB)

That night in the garden, Jesus spoke of a living trust for His bride, the church, that would secure her safekeeping, her joy, her holiness, and her eventual reunion with Him. The collective bride of Christ is made up of millions, perhaps billions, of women (as well as men). A natural man is required to care for only one woman the way Christ cared for many.

A ONE-WOMAN MAN

In a recent discussion with a friend of mine, we mused on the issue of whether Jesus could have ever married. We concluded that He could not, because He had too much love for everyone. He would not have been able to "leave and cleave" to just one. It would have been a departure from His nature to put one person above all others. Because He was the embodiment of love, it could not all have been contained by one woman. Plus He had a clear picture of His bride, the church, and He was willing to patiently wait for her, not settling for, or being distracted by, any other.

Some believe that men were not created to be monogamous, and women should accept the fact that they have to cheat. Yet God repeatedly commands a man to be committed to just one wife. In the list of biblical requirements for church leaders, the first is that the man should be the husband of one wife. Though extenuating circumstances might make a man who has remarried qualified for a leadership position in church, the perfect picture that God had in mind was that marriages would not be fractured or broken on the scale that they are today. To set an example for parishioners, the men in leadership should be as far above reproach as humanly possible.

Was Jesus strikingly handsome, the type of man who would make a maiden swoon? No, quite to the contrary. Isaiah 53:2 says, "in our eyes there was no attractiveness [about him] at all, nothing to make us want him" (TLB). Yet many women and men loved Him deeply. They were willing to die for Him, in fact, in order to share His love with others.

It was Christ's *inner* man that was beautiful beyond comparison, fairer than ten thousand. It was the things He said, the way He lived His life, His unadulterated caring, and His healing touch that moved the hearts of countless people who had the privilege of experiencing Him in the flesh. The memory of Him haunted them after His departure and lit their hearts on fire. They lived to please Him because of all He endured, suffered, and sacrificed for them.

As the ultimate husband, Jesus did not look for the reward to come from His bride. She *was* His reward. Anything that she failed to give would be made up for by the Father Himself. Jesus stayed focused on securing her heart and well-being in spite of her inconsistent moods and degrees of love, even upon finishing the work He knew He had to do to secure her future. Though her faith in Him had failed, He would rebuild her faith in Him. He would not leave her comfortless. Instead, He filled her arms with potent promises.

> I will not leave you as orphans; I will come to you. Before long, the world will not see me anymore, but you will see me. Because I live, you also will live. On that day you will realize that I am in my Father, and you are in me, and I am in you. Whoever has my commands and obeys them, he is the one who loves me. He who loves me will be loved by my Father, and I too will love him and show myself to him. (John 14:18-21)

> But the Counselor, the Holy Spirit, whom the Father will send in my name, will teach you all things and will remind you of

everything I have said to you. Peace I leave with you; my peace I give you. I do not give to you as the world gives. Do not let your hearts be troubled and do not be afraid. (John 14:26-27)

In my Father's house are many rooms; if it were not so, I would have told you. I am going there to prepare a place for you. And if I go and prepare a place for you, I will come back and take you to be with me that you also may be where I am. (John 14:2-3)

Jesus counted the cost and paid it. In spite of what would now separate Him from His bride, He made sure that she knew it was in body only, and that He went ahead to prepare the way for her to come into her own.

A man who walks and talks with God, who has the Spirit of God dwelling within him, is called to imitate Christ to the full measure in a marriage. He is called to count the cost before committing to a woman. When any breaches occur, he is called to take up the gauntlet, fight the dragon, and die to self in order to pursue reconciliation with his bride. He does his best to cover her offenses with his love, walking in integrity before God and man, believing that God will honor his obedience.

The nature of God's loving pursuit of His bride flies in the face of what we casually declare "irreconcilable differences."

As priest of the home, he purposes in his heart to cover his household with prayer and equip his family to meet the demands of life by giving them security and rest under his wings. Is this a lofty charge? Considering the limitations of human strength it would appear to be, but God will be strong in a man's weakness if given permission to be.

When a man submits himself to the process of becoming an imitator of God—when he lives a life of love, just as Christ loved us and gave Himself up for us as a fragrant offering and sacrifice to God (see Ephesians 5:1-2)—his wife will respond to his efforts with love and honor.

The nature of God's loving pursuit of His bride flies in the face of what we casually declare "irreconcilable differences" in order to gain a quick divorce. God says that He will not take His love from us or ever betray His faithfulness (see Psalm 89:33). He promises to maintain His love toward us forever and declares that His covenant with us will never fail (see Psalm 89:28). Though God's own bride has been adulterous at times, He has refused to give up on her. When the prophet Hosea was dealing with his adulterous wife, God told him, "Go, show your love to your wife again, though she is loved by another and is an adulteress. Love her as the LORD loves the Israelites, though they turn to other gods" (Hosea 3:1). God hates divorce and sees it as a last resort, so determined is He to fulfill His love commitment.

God's standard for love is one of consistency no matter what. In some cases, His standard will require you to sacrifice your pride as well as the dreams of how you thought that life should play out. If you find yourself unable to stand under crushing circumstances, please know that God will meet you with His grace wherever you are. If you *are* able to stand through the betrayal of your heart, God will restore the original picture of your life to a scene of even greater beauty in time.

To those whose flesh kicks and screams, "But you don't know what this person is taking me through!" God simply says, "My command is this: Love each other as I have loved you. Greater love has no one than this, that he lay down his life for his friends" (John 15:12-13). Or for his wife. Or for her husband.

THE ULTIMATE CHALLENGE

Single men and women, I hope this book has been a wake-up call for you to carefully consider the cost of commitment, the value of your potential partner, and your willingness to give all to love as Christ has called us to love. Are you ready to endure to the end—not just because it is a good thing for you to do, but because it glorifies the One who loves you most?

Married folks, consider this book my challenge to you to work out your differences. Jesus paid the cost to reconcile us to God when our relationship with Him was broken. Because of His shed blood, He has paved the way for us to have all that we need to bring restoration to our homes. What made it possible for the Proverbs 31 woman to be who she was? She had a husband who set a standard in the home as well as the marketplace. He released her to nurture the good in herself, which she gladly offered back to him.

The Proverbs 31 woman was not distracted by a man who forced her to manage a home he would not tend or to guard a heart he would not love. No. Their home was built on a solid rock, led and maintained by a godly man. His diligence ultimately released him to be the man he was called to be—an upstanding man in his community and a leader in his home. He was so confident in who he was that he could freely celebrate his wife's achievements and lead his children in calling her blessed. She could laugh at the future and have no worries because her heart was anchored in the Lord and in the trust she was able to place in her man.

Exercising the fruit of the Spirit, this amazing couple was "like-minded, having the same love, being one in spirit and purpose" (Philippians 2:2). Their like-mindedness fostered order in their home, which freed everyone who lived in it to be virtuous or excellent in all they determined to do.

What do you want your household to look like, O man of God, O woman of God? How the picture develops is up to you. You see, a wonderful relationship is not about you; it is about love. Out of love flow all the considerations that make a relationship work. Sometimes one person in the marriage will not have as much as he or she needs to cover the gap between spouses. The other must help repair the breach.

Though the man is called to bear the greater part of the burden (because of God's order for him to love his wife), the responsibility is still to be upheld by both. Paul encouraged the church with this exhortation that I think is a good one for married couples:

> Therefore, as God's chosen people, holy and dearly loved, clothe yourselves with compassion, kindness, humility, gentleness and patience. Bear with each other and forgive whatever grievances you may have against one another. Forgive as the Lord forgave you. And over all these virtues put on love, which binds them all together in perfect unity.
>
> Let the peace of Christ rule in your hearts, since as members of one body you were called to peace. And be thankful. (Colossians 3:12-15)

Is your heart totally sold out to the marital commitment that you have made? In spite of how His beloved sometimes fails to respond, Jesus has continued to keep His promise to her—to us. I believe the greatest attribute of the Proverbs 31 man was that he was a man who could be trusted. He was a mature man who stood behind his word and his commitment. After all, that is what separates the men from the boys and the guys from the gentlemen. A real man owns his promises and delivers them, driven not by the expectations of others but simply by love.

———

*May the Lord direct your hearts
into God's love and Christ's perseverance.*

2 THESSALONIANS 3:5

The Proverbs 31 man lives a life of unconditional love.

FOR REFLECTION AND DISCUSSION

For Him

"This is how we know what love is: Jesus Christ laid down his life for us. And we ought to lay down our lives for our brothers" (1 John 3:16). The husband is called to lay down his life for his wife. This is the ultimate act of love.

- What does love look like to you? What misconceptions from your past experiences have you harbored? How can you discover God's truth concerning these issues?
- What things do you do to promote love in your home? How do you reflect Christ to your loved ones?
- What does laying down your life look like to you? What rewards do you see yourself reaping from sacrificially loving your mate?
- How seriously are you committed to the vows you've made to your wife?
- Are you mature in your approach to love? In what ways do you need to grow?

For Her

"There is no fear in love. But perfect love drives out fear, because fear has to do with punishment. The one [man or woman] who fears is not made perfect in love. We love because he first loved us" (1 John 4:18-19). The woman can free her husband to love her unconditionally only by giving him her trust.

- If single, does the man you are considering for marriage display the capacity for mature love?
- If married, does your husband display mature love toward you?
- What are your personal issues concerning love? Are you able to receive love?
- What does love look like to you?
- In what ways do you mirror the love of Christ to your husband?

For You Both

- Are you willing to sacrifice your personal pleasure for the greater good of your relationship? Why or why not?
- Are you patient? How does this play out in your relationship with each other?
- Are you easily offended? If yes, why? How can you change your perspective on what you perceive as wrongs against you?
- Do you trust each other? Are your trust issues related to your own past experiences or to your mate's actions? How can you work together to nurture greater trust?
- What would God say about the way you love each other?

Who can find a man of integrity? For such a one is of priceless value that perpetually increases.

He walks in the fear of the Lord and observes all of His statutes.

He embraces wisdom wholeheartedly and continues in the way of sound discipline. He maintains discretion and does not depart from the path of righteousness, for he understands words of insight.

He treats his wife as he treats his own body, seeking her protection and well-being at all times.

The heart of his wife rests beneath his covering and flourishes in all fruitfulness under the outpouring of his love.

He is faithful, drinking from his own well, and is unceasingly satisfied by the wife of his youth, always loving her as a lover who loves still.

He will do her good and not evil all the days of his life. Though he waxes strong, he exercises humility.

He diligently works to answer and supply the needs of his family and household. His wife has no fear of the times to come, for he prudently considers the future and prepares for it.

He is kind to the needy, and his name is synonymous with a good report. His reputation precedes him; therefore, others seek his counsel and follow his example as well as instruction. His mouth is a fountain of life to his household and to all who seek refreshing.

He walks in confidence and sound judgment, administering wise instruction to his wife and children.

He sets his house in God-ordained order. He redeems his household and covers its inhabitants with prayer.

He considers the words of his wife, celebrates her wisdom, and crowns her as a helpmeet for him. He grants her a double portion, blesses her gifts, and boasts of her achievements.

He is clothed in love and faithfulness. He trusts and rests secure in the help of his Redeemer.

Many men appear to be desirable at first glance, but the man who fears the Lord is to be praised, for his witness endures the test of time and scrutiny. Give him the honor he has earned and let the work of his hands prosper and be spread abroad.

—*Michelle McKinney Hammond*

RECOMMENDED READING

Every Man's Battle by Stephen Arterburn and Fred Stoeker
Every Woman's Desire by Stephen Arterburn and Fred Stoeker
Intimate Issues by Linda Dillow and Lorraine Pintus
A Man After God's Own Heart by Jim George
The Master's Degree by Frank and P. Bunny Wilson
Maximized Manhood by Edwin Louis Cole
Men's Relational Toolbox by Gary, Greg, and Michael Smalley
Unmasking the Lone Ranger by Frank Wilson
What Makes a Man Feel Loved by Bob Barnes
Wild at Heart by John Eldredge

———

If you would like to correspond with Michelle or book her for a speaking engagement, contact her at:

Michelle McKinney Hammond
c/o HeartWing Ministries
P.O. Box 11052
Chicago, IL 60654
or log on to:
www.michellehammond.com

For speaking engagements, contact:
HeartWing Ministries
1-866-391-0955